ROYAL FRANKISH DIPLOMAS

Pepin I
King of Franks

Translated by: D.P. Curtin

Copyright @ 2023 Dalcassian Press

All rights reserved. No part of this publication may be reproduced, distributed, or transmitted in any form or by any means, including photocopying, recording, or other electronic or mechanical methods, without the prior written permission of the publisher, except in the case of brief quotations embodied in critical reviews and certain other non-commercial uses permitted by copyright law. For permission request, write to Dalcassian Press at dalcassianpublishing at gmail.com

ISBN: 979-8-3302-2621-4 (Paperback)

Library of Congress Control Number:
Author: Curtin, D.P. (1985-)

Printed by Ingram Content Group, 1 Ingram Blvd, La Vergne, Tennessee

First printing edition 2023.

ROYAL FRANKISH DIPLOMAS

ROYAL FRANKISH DIPLOMAS

I. CAPITULARY OF THE SON OF CHARLES MARTEL, ANNO 742.

In the name of our Lord Jesus Christ.

I, Carloman, leader and prince of the Franks, in the 742nd year from the incarnation of Christ, the 2nd month of May, with the counsel of the servants of God and my nobles, assembled the bishops who are in my kingdom with the presbyters, and the council and synod for the fear of Christ, that is, Boniface the archbishop. and Burghard, and Regenfrid, and Hwitan, and Vuillabald, and Dodanus, and Eddanus, together with their elders, that they might give me advice, how the law of God and the ecclesiastical religion, which had fallen in the days of the former princes, were destroyed, and how the Christian people should be saved for the soul. that he may be able to arrive, and that he may not perish deceived by false priests; and by the counsel of my priests and nobles we ordained bishops in the cities, and appointed over them the archbishop Boniface, who was sent by St. Peter. We decide to assemble a synod every year, so that the decrees of the canons and the rights of the church may be restored to us, and the Christian religion may be amended. And we restored and returned the defrauded funds of the churches to the churches. We removed and degraded false elders and adulterers or fornicators, deacons and clerics from the funds of the churches, and forced them to do penance.

2. We absolutely forbade the servants of God in all things to bear arms or to fight, or to go into exile and against the enemy, except only those who have been chosen for this because of the divine mystery, that is, to perform the solemnities of the masses, and to bear the patronage of the saints. That is, the leader should have one or two bishops with the chaplains of the priests, and each presbyter should have one presbyter, who can judge men who confess

their sins and tell them to repent. Nor have we forbidden all the servants of God those hunting and wild wanderings with dogs. In the same way that they do not have receivers and walkers.

3. We also decreed according to the canons of the saints, that every presbyter living in a parish should be subject to the bishop in whose parish he resides; and he must always render and show to the bishop the exact reason and order of his ministry, whether of baptism, or of the Catholic faith, or of prayers and the order of the masses. And whenever, according to canonical law, the bishop goes around the parish to strengthen the people, the presbyter should always be ready to receive the bishop, with the gathering and assistance of the people who need to be strengthened there. And at the Lord's Supper he should always seek a new confirmation from the bishop, so that the bishop may stand as a witness of his chastity, and of his life and faith and doctrine.

4. We decided that, according to canonical caution, we would not admit all unknown bishops or presbyters from wherever they came to ecclesiastical ministry before a synodal test.

5. We decreed that according to the canons each bishop should take care in his parish, with the help of the gravity of the defender of the church, that the people of God should not commit paganism, but that they should cast off and reject all the filthiness of gentiles; whether the sacrifices of the dead, whether of fortune-tellers or of the divine, whether phylacteries and auguries, whether incantations, or sacrificial victims, which foolish men perform near the churches in heathen rites, under the name of holy martyrs or confessors, provoking God and his saints to wrath; whether those sacrilegious fires, which they call nied fyr, or all, whatever they may be, they should carefully prevent the observation of the heathen.

6. We decreed likewise, that after this synod, which was on the 2nd of May, that any of the servants of God or handmaids of Christ who had fallen into the crime of fornication, should do penance in prison in bread and water. And if he had been ordained as a presbyter, let him remain in prison for two years, and

before that he should be seen scourged and flogged, and afterwards the bishop should be added. But if a cleric or monk has fallen into this sin, after the third whipping he is sent to prison, he must do penance there for the next year. In the same way, veiled nuns must be restrained by the same penance, and all the hair of their heads must be shaved.

7. We have also decreed that presbyters or deacons should not be sedated, after the manner of the laity, but should use huts, according to the rite of the servants of God. And no one will allow a woman to live in his house. And that the monks and handmaids of God should order and live according to the rule of Saint Benedict, they should strive to govern their own lives.

II. CAROLOMAN PRINCIPAL CAPITULAR, ANNO 743.

1. Now in this synodal assembly, which was assembled on the Month of March in a place called Liftinas, all the venerable priests of God and the counts and prefects of the former synod confirmed the decrees of the previous synod, agreeing to them, and promised to fulfill them and to observe them. And all the clergy of the ecclesiastical order, bishops and priests and deacons and clerics, accepting the canons of the ancient fathers, promised that they would recover ecclesiastical rights in morals and doctrines and in ministry. The abbots and monks received the rule of the Holy Father Benedict to restore the norm of regular life. Fornicators and adulterous clerics, who defiled holy places or monasteries before they were tenants, we command to remove them from there and to reduce them to penance. And if, after this definition, they have fallen into the crime of fornication or adultery, let them bear the judgment of the previous synod. Similarly, monks and nuns.

2. We have also decided with the counsel of the servants of God and the Christian people, because of the imminent wars and persecutions of other nations that are around us, that under a precarious and tax assessment some part of the ecclesial money for the help of our army with the indulgence of God will be retained for a certain time, on the condition that for years a solid, that is twelve denarii, shall be returned to the church or to the monastery; in such a

way that if he dies to whom the money was lent, the church is clothed with his own money. And again, if necessity compels the prince to order, the precarious one shall be renewed and a new one rewritten. And it must be absolutely observed that the churches or monasteries do not suffer want and poverty, whose funds are provided in a precarious manner. But if poverty compels, the whole possession shall be returned to the church and to the house of God.

3. Similarly, we order that according to the decrees of the canons, adulteries and incestuous marriages, which are not legitimate, should be prohibited and corrected by the judgment of the bishops; and that Christian slaves should not be handed over to pagans.

4. We also decided, as my father had previously ordered, that whoever made pagan observations in any matter should be fined and condemned to fifteen solidi.

III. PEPPIN'S PRINCIPLES CAPITULARY AT SOISSON, ANNO 744

In the name of God the Trinity. In the seven hundred and forty-fourth year from the incarnation of Christ under say the 5th of March and the 14th of the moon, in the second year of Childeric, king of the Franks, I, Peppin, leader and prince of the Franks. While many are not considered unknown, how we decided in the name of God, together with the consent of the bishops, or the council of priests or servants of God, or with the counts and generals of the Franks, to hold a synod or council at the city of Soisson: which we did in the name of God.

At first, we established the Catholic faith, which was established by 318 bishops in the Council of Nicaea, to be announced throughout our region, and the canonical judgments of other saints, which they established in their synods; how the law of God and the ecclesiastical rule, which had collapsed in the days of the former princes, were to be restored.

2. For this reason we, together with the consent of the bishops, whether priests or servants of God, and by the counsel of my superiors, have decided that we should renew the synod every year, so that the Christian people may reach the salvation of souls, and that heresy may no longer arise among the people, as we found in Adlaberto heresy, which was publicly condemned by 23 bishops with one voice; and many other priests, with the consent of the prince and the people, so condemned Adlabert himself, that the people should no longer perish, deceived by false priests.

3. For this reason, we established by the counsel of my priests and nobles, and ordained legitimate bishops in the states; therefore let us appoint over them the archbishops Abel and Ardobert, so that both the bishops and other people may have recourse to his or their judgments in every ecclesiastical necessity. That the order of monks or handmaids of God may remain stable according to the holy rule; and concerning ecclesiastical matters which have been neglected, the monks or the handmaids of God may be consoled, even to the point of satisfying their needs; and what he has exceeded, the tax is lifted. And let not the legitimate abbots make an opening, unless they transmit only their man. And all the clerics must not commit fornication, and they must not lead away the laity, nor do they hunt with dogs, nor carry receivers.

4. Similarly, we decreed that lay people should live lawfully, and not commit various forms of fornication, and not agree to perjury in the church, and not bear false witness, and preserve the church of God in every necessity. And let every priest who is in the parish be obedient and subject to the bishop, and always at the Lord's Supper give the account and order of his ministry to the bishop and ask for chrism and oil. And when, according to canonical law, the bishop goes round the parish to strengthen the people, the bishop, or the abbot, or the priest, should be ready to receive the bishop in aid of necessity.

5. And let us decide that bishops or priests coming from other regions are not to be accepted in the ministry of the church, unless they have first been approved by the bishop whose parish it is.

6. And we decided absolutely that every bishop in his parish should take care that the Christian people do not become pagans. And through all the commonwealth he may make lawful judgments and measures, according to the abundance of time.

7. Let us likewise arrange that those crosses which Adlabert had planted throughout the parish should all be consumed by fire.

8. Similarly, we have said that a cleric should not have a woman in his house to live with him, except his mother, or sister, or niece.

9. Let us similarly establish that no layman should have a woman consecrated to God as his wife, nor his own parent; neither shall another woman take her husband while he is alive, nor shall a woman take another while her husband is alive; for a husband ought not to divorce his wife, except when she is found guilty of fornication.

10. If anyone contrary to this decree, which the 23 bishops together with other priests or servants of God, together with the consent of the prince Peppin or the consuls of the Franks, have chosen to transgress or break the law, or have disapproved, let him be judged by the prince himself, or by the bishops, or by the counts. according to what is written in the law, each according to his order. And if we have observed all these things, which is written above, we shall be apt to find the mercy of Christ for ever and ever. Amen. + Sign of the inglorious man Peppin, of the house of the ancestors.

+ *The sign of Radobod*

+ *Aribert's sign*

+ *The sign of Helmigaud.*

IV. THE CAPITALARY OF KING PEPPIN IN VERMERIAN, ANNO 753.

1. In the third generation they are separated, and after penance, if they so wish, they have permission to join others. But if they are found in the fourth union, we do not separate them, but tell them to repent. However, if it has not been done, we do not give any possibility to join in the fourth generation.

2. If a man stays with his daughters, he can have neither his mother nor his daughter, and neither he nor she will be able to unite themselves to others at any time. However, if his wife so chooses, if she cannot control herself, if after she has learned that her husband was in adultery with her daughter, she does not have carnal intercourse with him, unless she abstains by will, she may marry another.

3. If a priest marries his niece, he must divorce her and lose his rank. If another receives it and rejects it from himself. If he cannot control himself, let him take another; because it is reprehensible that another man should have the relic of a priest.

4. In whatever way a woman has taken the veil, she should continue in it, unless someone has veiled herself against invitation or protest. Yet it must be preached that he may continue with his veil, if he will. But if the presbyter veiled her uninvited and remonstrated, he shall lose his rank for this cause. But if it happens that a woman presumes to cover herself without the consent of her husband, it will be in the power of her husband whether she continues in this or not.

5. If a woman has plotted the death of her husband with other men, and the husband himself kills the man in self-defense, and can prove this, that husband may divorce the wife herself, and if he wishes, take another. [And the plotter herself, having undergone penance, should remain without hope of marriage.]

6. If any innocent man has taken a slave wife as a virgin, if the woman herself has been enslaved afterwards, [if he can redeem her from slavery, let him do it]; if he cannot be redeemed, if he so chooses, let him receive another. In the same way, a virgin woman, if she accepts a slave as virgin, and afterwards he is served for whatever reason, unless he has sold himself due to want forced by hunger, and she has consented to this, and she has been freed from hunger by the price of her husband, she can, if she wishes, let him go, and if he cannot control himself, he cannot lead another. In the same way, if a woman has sold herself, and her husband has agreed to do so, he can stand in this way, if they have separated. Repentance, however, is necessary for both. For he who has been freed from such necessity at the expense of his partner, must continue in such a marriage, and not be separated.

7. If the servant has had a female concubine, if he so pleases, she may be freed and take her partner, the female slave of her master; but it is better to keep his handmaid.

8. If any servant, having received his freedom from his master, afterwards commits adultery with his handmaid, whether his master wills or not, he shall take her to wife. If he divorces her and marries another, he is absolutely compelled to divorce the latter and take back her with whom he first committed adultery, or else she should have no other while she lives.

9. If anyone, forced by unavoidable necessity, flees to another leadership or province, or follows his senior, to whom he cannot lie his faith; and his wife, when she is strong and able, through the love of her parents or of her property, will not follow him; she herself shall remain unmarried at all times, as long as her husband, whom she did not follow, lives. For that husband of hers, who is compelled by necessity to flee to another place [if he hopes never to return to his own country], if he cannot abstain, he may take another wife with penance.

10. If a son sleeps with his stepmother, his father's wife, neither he nor she can attain marriage. But that man, if he wishes, may have another wife; but it is better to abstain.

11. If a man has slept with his daughters, he may stand by a similar opinion; and he can stand with his wife's sister in a similar way.

12. He who sleeps with two sisters, and one of them was formerly his wife, shall have none of them; neither that adulterous sister, nor that man who committed adultery with her, should ever receive others.

13. He who knows that his wife is a slave, and has taken her willingly, must always continue with her afterwards.

14. That the ordination of presbyters should not be done by bishops traveling through the countries. But if those presbyters are good, they will be reaped again.

15. A degraded presbyter, compelled by certain necessity, on account of the danger of death, if no one else is present, may baptize the sick.

16. That clerics do not carry arms.

17. If any woman complains that her husband has never stayed with her, let them go from there to the cross; and if it be true, they shall separate, and she shall do as she pleases.

18. He who stays with his wife's cousin, let him be without his wife, and have no other. That woman he had, let him do what he will. The church does not accept this.

19. If a slave or a slave-girl has been separated by reason of sale, they are to be preached to remain so, if we cannot reunite them.

20. That the cartelier who has remained with a slave-girl, when, according to the law, having received her freedom from her master, has sent her away, taking another, let him release the latter.

21. He who has put away his wife to cover herself, shall not take another.

V. KING PEPPIN'S CAPITOLARY IN VERNENSE, ANNO 755

THE SYNOD BEGINS IN THE SPRING PALACE.

Indeed, the rules of the ancient fathers of the holy Catholic Church, the most correct norms promulgated for the correction of mortals, had been sufficient, if their most sacred rights had continued uninjured. But because some unsuited causes had arisen, and unsettled times had come on, it happened that some of these matters had been neglected by neglect, and therefore the most glorious and religious insolent man, Peppin, king of the Franks, caused almost all the bishops of the Gauls to assemble at the council of Vernus in the public palace, desiring for some time to recover the canonical institutions . And because the faculty is not fully capable, yet in some part he wants to be corrected, which he knows very well to be contrary to the Church of God. And if the serene times and quiet spaces have been bestowed upon him by God, he wishes to preserve them to the full according to the canons of the saints, more fully supplied by divine grace, better, more perfectly, and whole. And when this has been done, let these things, which have been forcibly removed from the sacred canons, cease, and let the aforesaid canonical rights remain intact and undefiled. However, in the meantime, as best as we can, we want these things to be undisturbed and inviolable. For the things themselves, which have been set forth for our common amendment, are kept inserted below by distinct chapters. He gives 20. This July, in the fourth year of the reign of our lord Peppin, the most glorious king.

1. That the bishops should be in each state.

2. The bishops whom we appointed in place of the metropolitans, that the other bishops should obey them in all things according to the canonical institution, meanwhile we amend this more fully according to the canonical constitution.

3. That each of the bishops should have power in his parish both over the clergy and over the regulars or laymen, to correct and amend according to the canonical spiritual order, so that they may live in such a way as to please God.

4. That a synod be held twice a year. The first synod in the first month, which is the month of March, when the king ordered his presence. The second synod on the Month of October, or at the Session or elsewhere where it meets on the Month of March among the bishops themselves. And let those bishops meet there, whom we have just appointed as metropolitans. And let the other bishops, or abbots, or presbyters, whom the metropolitan himself has ordered to come, cause to meet there in the second synod itself.

5. That the monastics, both men and women, should live regularly according to the order of the saints. And if they disdain to do this, the bishop in whose parish they appear to be should correct this. And if he cannot, let him know whom we have appointed metropolitan, and he himself will make amends. And if even he himself could not amend this, let them come from thence to a public synod, and there he should receive the canonical opinion. And if he scorns the public synod, he shall either lose his honor, or be excommunicated by all the bishops, and such a person shall be appointed in his place in the synod itself, by the word and will of the lord the king, or by the consent of the servants of God, who according to the holy order governs the flock itself.

6. We decreed that no abbess should presume to have two monasteries, nor should she be permitted to go outside the monastery, except by force of hostility. But the lord the king says that he wishes that when the lord the king himself has ordered some of the abbesses to come to him, once a year and with the consent of the bishop in whose parish he is, that then some should come to him, and by his own command, if need be, and elsewhere he ought not at all to

tarry in the villages [or in other] places, except only when he can walk and return more quickly. And he did not move from his monastery until he had sent his message to the king. And if the king commanded him to come, let him come. If, however, he remains in the monastery, in the meantime we amend this more fully according to the canons. Similarly, those nuns should not go outside the monastery. But if anyone has fallen in any slip, he must do penance in the monastery below by the advice of the bishop. And if it is necessary to suggest something concerning their necessity to the lord the king or to the synod, their ambassadors or envoys should do this. And what kind of gifts they wish to give to the palace, let them direct this through their messengers. And if there are any monasteries which have not been able to fulfill their order because of poverty, let that bishop foresee this in truth, and let this lord the king know, that he may make amends for this in his alms. And if such veiled women are found gathered there for the time being, who do not wish to live regularly, and are not worthy to live with them elsewhere, the bishop or the abbess must provide a suitable place, where they must live separately with the guard in the pulsation, or work with their hands as the abbess herself He commanded, in the meantime, that those who had been approved, if they were worthy, should be received in the congregation.

7. That there should not be a public baptistery in any parish, except where it has been established by the bishop whose parish it is. Except only if the necessity arises because of infirmity, or because of necessity, those priests whom the bishop has appointed in the parish itself, in whatever place it happens, have permission to baptize, so that they do not die without baptism at all.

8. Of the priests. That all the priests who are in the parish should be under the authority of the bishop of their order, and that no presbyter should presume to baptize or celebrate masses in that parish without the command of the bishop in whose parish he is. And let all the presbyters come together to the council of the bishop. And if they contemn to do this which is understood above, they shall be judged according to the canonical institution, both they and their defenders.

9. Of the methods of excommunication, both of clerics and laymen. If any presbyter has been degraded by his bishop, and through contempt he afterwards presumes to do something about his office without provision, and is afterwards reprimanded and excommunicated by the bishop, who has knowingly communicated with him, let him know that he has been excommunicated. Similarly, whoever, cleric, layman, or woman, has committed incest, and when reproved by his bishop, refuses to amend, and is excommunicated by him, whoever communes with him shall likewise be excommunicated. And that you may know what is the manner of this excommunication, he must not enter the churches, nor take fish or drink with any Christian; he must neither accept his gifts, nor extend a kiss, nor join in prayer, nor greet him, until he has been reconciled by his bishop. But if anyone complains that he has been unjustly excommunicated, he shall have permission to come to the metropolitan bishop, and there he shall be judged according to the canonical institution; and in the meantime he should keep his excommunication. But if anyone despised all these things, and the bishop was not able to correct this in the least, he would be condemned to exile by the king's judgment.

10. That monks who live truthfully and regularly should not be allowed to wander to Rome or elsewhere unless they exercise obedience to their abbot. And if such a cause should happen, that he is absent, that the abbot is found neglected or neglected, or that the monastery itself falls into the hands of the laity, and this the bishop will not be able to remedy, and there were some such monks there who, for God's sake, would want to migrate from the monastery to another for the sake of their souls. to be saved, let them have permission from their bishop, how they can save their souls.

11. Concerning those men who say that they shave themselves for God's sake, and only have their goods or money, and are neither under the hand of the bishop, nor live in a regular monastery, it was agreed that they should be in the monastery under the regular order, or under the hand of the bishop under the order canonical And if they do otherwise, and when corrected by their bishop, refuse to amend, they shall be excommunicated. And the same form shall be preserved of the veiled handmaids of God.

12. In the canon of Chalcedon, chapter 20. On not receiving clerics of another church and on those receiving them without letters of recommendation. Clergy serving in churches, as it has already been established, are not permitted in the church of another state or in the military power of the laity, but to continue in the place where the principle merited to minister; besides those who, having lost their country, came to another church out of necessity. But whoever of the bishops or laymen received a cleric of another church after this, except to excuse himself reasonably, it was decided to be suspended from communion, and he who receives, and he who was received, as long as the cleric who was transferred, did not return to his own church. Codd. 2 and 3 proceed as follows:

13. Concerning vacant bishops, who have no parishes, and we do not know what their ordination was like, it was decided according to the institutions of the holy fathers, that they should not minister in another's parish, nor perform any ordination without the command of the bishop whose parish it is. And if he presumes to do this, he shall be suspended from office in the meantime that he comes to the synod from there, and there he shall receive a sentence according to the canonical institution, except only for the purpose of the journey. And if any cleric or layman defends such a bishop or priest without the support of the bishop whose parish he belongs to, he shall be excommunicated until he makes amends.

14. On Sunday, because the people are persuaded, that on Sunday one should not travel with horses, as well as oxen and carts, nor prepare anything for food, nor do anything pertaining to the splendor of the house or of man, which matters are more a matter of Jewish superstition than of Christian superstition. it is proved that the observation is relevant, we decide that on Sunday, what was allowed to be done before, may be allowed. However, we have decided to refrain from agricultural work, plowing, or cutting vineyards, shaking, girdling, or hedges, so that those who come to church may more easily be freed from the grace of prayer. If anyone is found to be engaged in the above-mentioned works which are forbidden, how he should make amends, it should not consist in the division of the laity, but in the chastisement of the priests.

15. That all lay people should perform public weddings, both noble and ignoble.

16. From the canon of Chalcedon ch. 3. That clerics should not be employers, that is, that they should not have any secular activity, except for the causes of the churches of orphans or widows, by the order of their bishop [or abbot].

17. From the canon of Chalcedon ch. 25. that after the death of a bishop it is not permitted to be an episcopate without a pastor for more than three months; unless such a great necessity arises that this cannot be done in any way. Especially when the next synod takes place, a bishop will be ordained.

18. That no cleric should attend public lay courts without the order of his bishop or abbot, according to the canon of Carthage, chapter 8, as it is written there: loses This in a criminal trial. But in the civil state he must lose what he has driven away, if he wishes to take his place. For he who has the authority to elect judges from all sides of the church judges himself unworthy of the fraternal association who, feeling bad about the whole church, asks for help from a secular judgment, when the apostle orders the cases of private Christians to be deferred to the church and terminated there. And above all, that in such cases he should not make his lord the king uneasy.

19. Concerning immunities, that all immunities may be preserved throughout all the churches.

20. In another synod you forgave us those monasteries where monks or nuns regularly lived, so that you let them know about those things where they could live, so that from then on, if he was royal, he made abbots or abbesses of reason for the lord king: and if episcopal, to that bishop. In the same way about those villages.

21. That those presbyterates which obtain the episcopate by laws, that those bishops ought to have them themselves, as you said before in another synod.

22. Concerning the pilgrims who go for God's sake, so that they do not levy taxes on themselves; and with regard to other publicans, as you have pardoned, let it be so, that they may pass where they have not been lawfully given.

23. That the counts or judges, at their pleasure, may at first hear or determine the cases of widows, orphans, or churches in alms to the king, and afterwards other cases may be reasonably judged by justice.

24. That no one should approach ecclesiastical rank or honor through money, because it seems to be a simonian heresy.

25. That no bishop, nor abbot, nor layman, for the sake of justice, should accept a sport that is contradicted; because where the gifts themselves conflict, justice is voided.

VI. KING PEPPIN'S CAPITALARY IN COMPENDIENSE, ANNO 757

BEGINNING OF THE DECREE WHICH WAS MADE FOR THE COMPENSATION OF THE PUBLIC PALACE.

1. If they are found united in the fourth generation, we do not separate them.

2. But in the third, if they are found, they shall be separated.

3. And those which belong to one in a fourth, and another in a third, and are found joined together, we separate.

4. If two belong to each other in the third place, either male or female, or one in the third and the other in the fourth; When one is dead, it is not permissible for

the other to take his wife. And if they are found, they shall be separated. There is one law for men and for women.

5. If a woman puts a veil on her head without her husband's provision, if it pleases her husband, let him take her back to the marriage.

6. And if a man gives his daughter Franca, against the wishes of himself and his mother and parents, to a simple man, or a servant or an ecclesiastic, and she refuses to have him, and leaves him, her parents have the power to give her another husband. And if she has another, whom she later married, they shall not be separated.

7. If a Frank man takes a woman, and hopes that she is virgin, and afterwards finds that she is not virgin, let him divorce her if he wishes, and marry another. In the same way a woman is born.

8. If a woman has married a slave in virginity, and she knew then that he was a slave, let her live in the meantime. There is one law for men and women.

9. A Frankish man received a boon from his elder, and brought his vassal with him, and afterwards the elder himself died there, and released the vassal himself there; and after this another man received the same boon, and in return for this, that he might better have that vassal, he gave him a woman from the boon himself, and he had her for some time. and having dismissed her, he returned to the parents of his dead elder, and took a wife there, and now has her. It is defined that he has the same woman whom he later received.

10. If a man, having taken a wife, finds her defiled by his brother, divorces her and marries another, and finds her defiled, his wife is legitimate, because he was not a virgin at that time. But if he afterwards receives a third, he shall return to the median; and the latter herself has the power to unite herself to another man.

11. If a man has a legitimate wife, and his brother has committed adultery with her, that brother or that woman who committed adultery shall never have a spouse during the time they live. He whose wife he was, if he wills, has the power to take another.

12. If a person is baptized by an unbaptized priest, and the Holy Trinity is invoked in the baptism itself, he is baptized, as Pope Sergius said. However, he needs the imposition of the bishop's hands:

13. If a father has oppressed his son's bride, and afterwards the son has taken her, his father shall not have a wife afterwards, and the woman herself shall not have a husband, because she did not say that her father had stayed with her; but the son of him who did it unknowingly, let him take a legitimate wife.

14. In whatever way a woman has voluntarily taken the holy veil, she must remain in it and not let it go. George the Roman bishop and John the priest agreed.

15. If a man holds a son or daughter-in-law before the bishop for confirmation, he shall separate from his wife, and shall not take another. Similarly, the woman should not accept the other.

16. If a man divorces his wife and gives provisions for religious purposes to serve God below the monastery, or gives permission to veil herself outside the monastery, as we have said, for God's sake, her husband should take a legitimate wife. Let the woman do likewise.

17. If a man has remained in adultery with his mother and daughter, the mother not knowing that he had remained with her daughter, and likewise the daughter did not know that she was with her mother, then if that man has taken a woman, let him divorce her, and he shall not have a wife until the day of his death, and she let the woman whom he has left take her husband; and that mother and daughter, with whom she remained in adultery, both of them not

knowing that she had remained with mother and daughter, had husbands. For if this crime comes to their knowledge, let them divorce their husbands and do penance, and let their husbands take their wives after them.

18. In the same way about two sisters, with one of whom he remained in adultery and married the other in public, he must not have a wife until the day of his death. And those two sisters, if they did not know, should have husbands. And if it comes to their notice, let them keep the above form.

19. If a leprous man has a healthy woman, if he wishes to give her provisions so that she may receive a husband, the woman herself, if she wishes, may receive it.

20. If a man married a woman and had her for some time, and the woman herself says that he did not stay with her, and the man says that he did so, let the truth of the man stand, because he is the head of the woman. Concerning the woman who says that her husband has not returned her marital intercourse.

21. If those who, on account of feud, flee to another country, and divorce their wives, neither those men nor those women shall accept marriage.

22. Of incest. If a man commits incest with his mother, or with his mother from his source and confirmation, or with mother and daughter, or with two sisters, or with a brother's or sister's daughter, or with a niece, or with a cousin or niece, or with an aunt or aunt, on these charges he shall lose his money, if he has any. And if he refuses to make amends, no one will receive him, nor give him food. And if he does, he shall pay 60 solids to the king's house, until the man himself corrects himself. And if he has no money, if he is free, let him be sent to prison until satisfaction. If he is a slave or a freedman, he shall be beaten with many stripes. And if his master permits him to fall into such a crime any longer, the master himself shall make up to the king 60 solids.

23. As for ecclesiastics, if he has been a good person, he must lose his honor. But the minors are flogged and sent to prison.

24. Regarding priests and clerics, we order that the bishop's archdeacon should recall them to the synod together with the count. And if anyone blasphemes, the count shall have him disbarred, and the priest himself or his defender shall pay 40 solids, and he shall come to the synod. And the bishop himself causes the priest or cleric to be judged according to canonical authority; but he composes 40 solids. And if any one by violence contradicts a priest, or a cleric, or an incestuous person, then the earl shall cause the person himself to come before the king, together with the bishop's messenger, placed by sureties; and let the lord the king separate, that the rest may be redeemed.

VII. CONVENTION RELATING TO THE LAW, ANNO 765

The names of the bishops, or abbots, who hold the public town of Attinia for the cause of exile and the salvation of souls, having been gathered together in a synodal meeting, among other things, healthily and wisely defined, they also decreed this common council by decree, that every one of those whose names are found written below in this index, when any one has emigrated from this world , a hundred psalteries and his priests sing a hundred special masses. But the bishop himself should perform 30 masses; unless prevented by infirmity or some infirmity. Then he asks another bishop to sing for him; but the abbots who are not bishops, ask the bishops to perform the 30 masses in their turn, and their presbyters remember to play a hundred masses and the monks a hundred psalteries. Hrodeganus, bishop of the city of Mettis. Eddo, bishop of the city of Strasburg. Lullo, bishop of the city of Maguntia. Wolf bishop of the city of Senoni. Baldeberht, bishop of the city of Basel. Uulframnus, bishop of the city of Meldis. Remedius was called bishop of the city of Rodoma. Maurinus, bishop of the city of York. Genbaudus, bishop of the city of Laudum. Hildiganus, bishop of the city of Suaseon. Athalfridus, bishop of the city of Novius. Megingozus, bishop of the city of Wirziaburg. Bishop William of the monastery of Saint Maurice. Folricus, bishop of the city of Tungri. Theodulfus, bishop of the monastery of Laubici. Hiddo, bishop of the city of Agustoduno. Ippolitus, bishop of the monastery of Eogendi. Jacob, bishop of the monastery of Gamundias. Gaucilenus, bishop of the city of Celmani. John, bishop of the city of Constantia. Bishop Willibald of the monastery of Achistad. Madalpheus, bishop of the city of Wirdun. Harifeus, bishop of the city of Bisention. Leodeningus, bishop of the city of Baiogas. Eusebius, bishop of the city of Toron. Tello, bishop of the city of Goeradiddo. Mauriolus, bishop of the city of Andecavi. Fulradus, abbot of the monastery of St. Dionisius. Lanfrid, abbot of St. Germanus. John, abbot of St. Flodoald. Druhtgangus, abbot of Gemedico. Abbot of Withlecus of Funtanella. Abbot Witmar of Centula. Leodarius, abbot of Corbeia. Manasses, abbot of Flaviniacus. Asinarius, abbot of Novalicio. Waldo, abbot of St. John. Fabigaud, abbot of Busbrunn. Godobert, abbot of Rasbaci. Athalbert, abbot of Fabaria. Widradus, abbot of Saint Columba. Ebarsindus, abbot of Aldaha. Geraus, abbot of Niviella. Ragingarius, abbot of Utica.

VIII. KING PEPPIN'S CAPITALARY OF AN UNCERTAIN YEAR.

CHAPTER BEGINNING OF ANOTHER SYNOD HELD UNDER KING PEPPIN

In the first chapter of incest. If a man commits incest for these reasons, consecrated by God, or with his concubine, or with a spiritual mother from the source and confirmation of the bishop, or with a mother and daughter, or with two sisters, or with a brother's daughter, or a sister's daughter, or a niece, or with A cousin or niece, or with an aunt or uncle, shall lose his money, if he has any, for these crimes; and if he refuses to make amends, no one shall receive him, nor give him food. And if he does [this], he shall pay 60 solids to the king's house, until the man himself corrects himself. And if he has no money, if he is free, let him be sent to prison until satisfaction. If he be a slave or a freedman, he shall be beaten with many stripes. And if his lord has allowed him to fall [more] into such a crime, he shall make up [themselves] 60 solidi to the king's lordship.

2. As for ecclesiastics who have committed the aforesaid crimes, if they have been good persons, let them lose their honor; but the minors are flogged, or shut up in prison.

3. Regarding the priests and clerics, we order that the archdeacon of the bishop should recall them to the synod together with the count. And if anyone

blasphemes, the count shall cause him to be disbarred, so that the priest or his defender himself shall pay 60 solidi, and go to the synod. And the bishop himself should cause the priest or cleric to be judged according to canonical authority. The solid 60 should come to the king's chapel for the same reason. And if any one by violence contradicts a priest, or a cleric, or an incestuous person, then the count himself, having been placed before the king by sureties, shall cause him to come together with a messenger to the bishop; and let the lord the king disband, that the rest may be redeemed.

4. As regards tolls, we order them in such a way that no one should collect tolls from provisions or carriages, which are without business. In the same way, wherever they go, and pilgrims, who for God's sake are going to Rome or anywhere else, we have appointed them in the same way, so that you do not on any occasion detain them at the bridges and gates or by boat, nor do you make a complaint to any stranger because of their sloppiness, nor do you levy any toll on them. And if anyone does this, no matter what kind of person proves this, we grant him thirty of the 60 solidi, and let those others come to the king's chapel.

5. Regarding the coin, we decided that he should no longer have in the weighing balance but 22 solidi, and that the minter should take 1 solidi out of the 22 solidi, and return the others to their owner.

6. That immunities may be preserved.

7. Of justice to be done, that all may do justice, both public and ecclesiastical. And if a man comes to the palace for his own cause, and he has not previously introduced himself to that count in the mall before the Rachemburgs, or if his cause was before the count in the mall before the Rachemburgs, and he refuses to bear this because they themselves have judged him legitimately; if he comes to the palace for the same reasons, he will be flogged. And if he be a greater person, it shall be at the discretion of the king. And if he protested that they had not judged the law for him, then he should have permission to come to the palace for his own cause. And if he can convince them that they did not judge

him according to the law, let him make amends against him according to the law. And if the count or the members of the Racheburg could convince him that they had passed the law to him, and he would not accept this, let him make amends against them. In the same way, the ecclesiastics, if they came to the palace to complain about their cause against their elder, were to be beaten, unless their elder went over for his own cause.

ENCYCLICAL ON MAKING LETANIES.

Peppin, by the grace of God, king of the Franks, a illustrious man, lord the holy father bishop Lullus. We know that your sanctity has known what kind of piety and mercy God has shown in the present year in that land. He gave tribulation for our transgressions, and after the tribulation great and wonderful comfort, or the abundance of the fruits of the earth, which we now have. And for this and for our other reasons we need to thank him, because he was pleased to comfort his servants through his mercy. Thus, it seems to us that, without the prescribed fast, every bishop in his parish makes litanies, not with fasting, but only in praise of God, who has given us such abundance; and let every man do his alms and feed the poor. And so, make provision and order concerning our word, that every man, whether willing or unwilling, may give his tithe. Farewell in Christ.

IX. KING PEPPIN'S CAPITALARY OF AQUITAINE, ANNO 768

THE CHAPTERS BEGIN WITH WELL MEMORY OF PEPPIN, THE GENEALOGIST OF SINODALITES, AND WE WISH TO PRESERVE FROM MEN.

1. That those churches of God which are deserted may be restored, both by bishops and abbots, or by those lay men who benefit from them.

2. That those bishops, abbots, and abbesses may live under the holy order.

3. That whatever bishops, abbots or abbesses, or the rest of the priests have of the affairs of the churches for their use, may possess in a quiet order, as was already established in our synod; and if any one subsequently took anything away from it, he must return it in full.

4. That they should not take more from those poor people than they should legally pay.

5. Whoever has our benefice, let him work hard there; and he who does not wish to do this, let him let go of the benefit itself, and let him keep his own property.

6. Whoever goes on a journey, either hostilely or by agreement, should not take anything on his equal, unless he has been able to buy or provide, except grass, water and wood; but if such a time has been, no one forbids residence.

7. Whoever, while he has been with us, has taken away or forced anything on his own account, let him restore it threefold according to his own law.

8. If any man should protest before us, let him have leave to come to us, and let no one detain him by force.

9. Concerning those benefits for which the intention is, we want them to have those to whom we previously gave them.

10. That all men should have their law, both Roman and Salic, and if he came from another province, he should live according to the law of his own country.

11. That all the laymen and seculars who hold the things of the church, may receive from them precarious things.

12. That whatever our messengers may have agreed with those elders of the country for our progress or for the better of the holy church, let no one presume to dispute this. It is clear that the chapters of Peppin will be composed [sometime].

X. The plea of king Peppin, by which the town of Abaciacum, the village of Cenomanici and the portion of Sibriaci, is claimed by the Dionysian monks of Matriacen (in the year 752).

Peppin, king of the Franks, was a illustrious man. When we, in the name of God Vermeria, resided in our palace together with our nobles or faithful to hear the causes of the universe or to terminate them with a just judgment; there, the venerable man Fulradus, the abbot, coming from the basilica of the special patron of our lord Dionysius, where the precious lord himself rests in body, interrupted a certain man named Gislemarus, retrieving from him a certain village of St. Dionysius, which is called Abaciacus, in the village of Cenomanius, or also of Oximensi. even that portion in Sibriac in the Matriacens, which a certain woman, named Joba, the mother of Gislemar himself, had brought by her will to the aforesaid house of St. Dionysius of the same town before King Chilpericus, the owner of the property, Gislemarus himself retained in bad order and unjustly. But Gislemarus himself stood by at the present time, so that he could not at all deny it: but at the present time he recognized that his mother-in-law, Joba, had condoned the very town of Abaciacum above mentioned with all its integrity in the village of Matriacens to the house of St. He was seen to have recovered his wadi from the above-mentioned villages of Abaciacus and Sibriacus, that is, from all that the above-mentioned Joba, his mother-in-law, had donated to the house of St. Dionysius, or had held in the villages themselves; afterwards, by means of his feast, he said that from that point on he was against the abbot Fulradus himself in the cause of St. Dionysius. Accordingly, we judged that we together with our nobles or faithful, that is, Milo, Rotgarius, Helmengand, Chrothard, Charichard, Autgarius, and Wicbert, count of our palace, or the rest, as many as were seen; as because Gislemarus himself was in the present, and could not give any reason; therefore we order that, since this cause has been thus acted or perpetrated, Fulradus the abbot himself or his successors the very towns named above, Abaciacum with all its integrity and with all its adjacencies or appendages, whole and to the whole, a thing unclaimed; or also Sibriac in the village of Matriacens, that is, together with the lands, the houses superimposed upon them, the farms, the farms, the vineyards, the woods, the fields, the meadows, the pastures, the waters, or the streams; vineyards or sub-vineyards, flour mills, flocks with shepherds of both genders and sexes, and whatever Joba donated by his will to the house of St. Dionysius, or already before King Chilpericus, our ancestor, and Hugh himself, the ancestor of the abbot of Fulradius, the auctrix had, after examining the wills themselves, against Gislemarus himself vindicated and eliminated: and let there be a cause between them in the future from this matter at all times dormant.

Given in the month of March, in the first year of our reign.

XI. The order of King Peppin obtained by Sigobald, the abbot of Anisolensis (anno 752).

To the holy and apostolic lords and venerable fathers in Christ, to all the bishops and abbots, counts, domestics, vicars, centenarians, or to all our agents, both present and future, your illustrious man Peppinus, king of the Franks, wishing you well.

May your charity or your energy be satisfied, because Sigobald, abbot of the monastery of Anisola, which was built in honor of St. Carileph the confessor, in the village of Cenomanico, in the province of Labrocinse, has come to us, and of his own power himself and that holy congregation which he has under his government. and he more fully commended all their matters into our hands; and with a grateful heart we received and retained him and his congregation in our Mundeburdo. let him not enter, unless the holy congregation themselves choose from among themselves, let them have the abbot himself. For this reason, we have given our letters, sealed with our own hand, to him, through whom [which] we absolutely request and command you that neither you, nor your juniors or successors, disturb or condemn the abbots of His place, nor the mercy of their power, nor men who seem to hope through these laws. nor to abstract from their affairs nor to diminish them, unless, as we have said, it is permitted for them to live or reside in a more peaceful order under our protection or defense, and to implore the mercy of the Lord more attentively for us. if they have risen up their men, who have not been properly and reasonably defined in the village without their expenses, let them be suspended or locked up in every way until before us; and afterward they should receive judgment before us by law and justice; and that you may believe more assuredly, we have sealed it with our own hand, and sealed it with our ring.

The sign of Peppin, king of the Franks.

Chrodingus acknowledged the order.

Given on April on the 25th day of the first year of the reign of King Peppin. Acted at the public palace of Arestal.

XII. The royal decree of Peppin under Boniface concerning the affairs of the church of Saint Martin (in the year 753).

Peppin, king of the Franks. Let it be known to all our agents, both present and future: It behooves the Principal to lend a kind ear to all acts of clemency, especially when we prove by the summary of the souls of our previous kings and princes that our parents have been canceled to the places of the churches, we must weigh with a devout mind, and appropriate benefits, so that we deserve to be partakers of the reward, not to deny, but to confirm with the strongest right our oracles Therefore the apostolic man and father in Christ, Boniface, bishop of the city of Trajetensis, suggested to our royal clemency, that our ancestors, or parents, Clotharius, once king, and Theodebert, once signed by their hands, of the villas of the church of St. Martin which he presently possessed, or of by the fact that it had been previously delegated there by God-fearing men, they had granted it intact and unimpaired, so that no public judge could hear cases, or demand restraints, nor make mansions or prepare them, nor take away sureties, nor separate the men of the church itself for any reason, nor require any redistribution , they should not enter there; whence the very precepts of the princes already mentioned, or the confirmations of those kings, strengthened by their hands, the aforesaid priest Boniface shows us to be repelled, and the very benefice concerning the same church of St. Martin, as it was canceled by the aforesaid princes, asserts to have been preserved in modern times. But for the sake of firmness, he asked our highness that our authority should once again confirm this in general regarding the same church of St. Martin mentioned above. Know whose request for the reverence of the holy place itself, that we may deserve to be associated with the reward, we have seen the fullest willingness to grant, or to confirm in all things. We therefore command those in command that, as is clear from the aforesaid princes of the towns of the aforesaid church. Martin was granted complete immunity without the entrance of the judges; so that with the help of the Lord in the past, the authorities of the former princes may be preserved in every way, and neither you, nor your juniors and successors, nor anyone from the judicial power into the towns of the aforesaid church, which in modern times are known to possess anywhere in our kingdom, or have formerly been there by God-fearing men collated or collated, both of the innocent and of the servants, or of any nation of men residing in the aforesaid towns of the church itself, which shall legitimately return to the episcopate itself or to the church of St. Martin itself at the legitimate beginning, neither to hear cases, nor to demand relief, nor to remove sureties, neither mansions nor preparations to be made, nor the men of the church itself to be separated for any reason, nor to enter without presuming to require any redistribution; may the superfluities upon this authority of ours remain perpetually undisturbed by a general confirmation in the name of God, and that whatever our treasury could hope for in the lights of the church may forever prosper in increases, and that this authority may be evident both in present and future times, God the Helper, under it We decided to strengthen it with our own hands.

The sign of the glorious Peppin, king of the Franks.

XIII. Order of King Peppin for the monastery of Morbac (in the year 753).

Peppin, king of the Franks, a man of renown. It behooves the principle of clemency to lend a kind ear, especially for the saving of souls from our previous kings and predecessors to the places of the churches. but to confirm with the strongest right for our oracles. Therefore Baldebert, a venerable man, by the gift of God, abbot of the monastery of Vivario-Peregrino, which is placed in a village in Alsace above the river Morbac, which was built in honor of Saint Leodegar and Saint Peter the Apostle and Saint Mary and the rest of the saints, where he is known to serve with a large crowd of monks, the clemency of the kingdom He suggested ours by the fact that our ancestors had once by their authority signed with their hands the villages of the holy church itself, which [which] he possessed at the present time, both from the gifts of the princes, or from Eberhard, who founded the monastery himself with his alms, and from the generosity of the peasants, or that previously It was delegated there by God-fearing men, that they had granted with complete immunity, that no public judge should act in the towns or in the affairs of their own church, neither to hear cases, nor to exact fines, nor to make mansions or make ready, nor to remove sureties, nor men of the church itself for any causes to be cut off, nor to require any retribution, let him not dare to enter there. Hence the very precept to our forefathers already mentioned, or the aforesaid abbot Baldebert, the rector of the monastery himself, shows us their confirmation for relegation, and he asserts that the benefice itself has been preserved around the same mentioned church of his until now. But for the sake of stability, he asked our highness to confirm this once more about the monastery itself or about the monks themselves, our authority in general. Whose petition for the reverence of the place itself, that we may deserve to be associated with the reward, we were seen to have granted with the fullest willingness; or know that he has confirmed in all things. We therefore command the presiding officers that no public judge should be involved in the affairs or resources of the church itself, neither to hear cases, nor to demand reliefs, nor to make mansions or make ready, nor to take away sureties, nor men of the church itself, so naive as slaves, who seem to be commanding over their lands even at first, who are looking there, should not be separated from [him] for any reasons, nor require any retribution, should not enter there. But just as his benefice was canceled by our predecessors as already mentioned, it was preserved until now by the authority of the former princes to the church as already mentioned, so it will remain generally unshakable from now on by our authority. And whatever our treasury could hope for from thence, in the luminaries of Lord Leodegarius himself and of St. Peter, or of St. Mary, for the stability of our kingdom, may it proceed to increase. And in order that this authority may be evident in both present and future times, we have confirmed it with our hand below, and ordered it to be sealed with our ring.

XIV. The diploma of King Peppin for the Feast of St. Dionysius (in the year 753).

Peppin, king of the Franks, was an illustrious man. To all the captains, counts, scribes, domestics, vicars, centenarians, or all agents both present and future, or all our messengers running everywhere from the palace. Therefore, let your usefulness or greatness know that the venerable man Foleradus, abbot of the basilica of our special patron Saint Dionysius, where the precious lord himself with his companions seems to be resting in body, or that the abbot himself and a large company of monks seem to dwell in the same convent, or that they are known as a military lord. In a mass petition they suggested to us that a long time ago the kings Dagobert and Chlodius, or afterwards Hildericus and Theudericus, and Clotarius, formerly kings, and also Hilbertus, and our uncle Grimoaldus, the eldest of the house, and themselves once killing all the publicans in the village of Parisiaco The Saxons, as well as the Frisians, or other promiscuous nations from which villages or provinces to the festival of St. Dionysius the Martyr, both in the city itself and in the city of Paris itself for the purpose, or through the villages, or through the fields, both there and elsewhere to kill. or to carry out a great deal of carnage, and to procure wine in the ports, and by different rivers, who had come to the festival itself, so that the tax-collector himself, in integrity, from the very turn to the house of St. Dionysius, had conceded, or confirmed; to read Having read and gone through the precepts themselves, or confirmations, or by that judgment vindicated by Lord Hilbert, king and our uncle Grimoald the Great House, whom the agents of St. Dionysius claimed over the infamous man Grimoald the Great House, they presented him to us for banishment. And afterwards Folradus himself suggested to the abbot, or to the monks of St. Dionysius, and this they said, that the tax-collector of that mark in the towns or their fields, without any judges, should attend the entrance to the house of St. Dionysius; with greed, and Gairefred the Count of Paris lying in wait, by their consent killing or branding them, they had made each honest man to give four dinars by supplication, and this they took from them in bad order. And afterwards Gairehard, the Count of Paris, or acting as his agents, as they found there by custom, exacted this upon the men themselves, and upon every innocent man of whatever nation who came to that mark, they exacted four dinars from their head, if he was innocent; and if he was a slave, then he had to swear that he had been a slave, and the people themselves, when they swore by the very sacrament, gave five dinars for this. And when Saint Dionysius did this, or Folradus the Abbot, or those monks, they said that by such a custom that Markadus had been removed or abstracted, and that those killing or all the nations that were wont to come to the Markadus, for this reason fled from the Markadus himself, and that publican from the same God's house was small or abstract. And Gairehardus himself said this, that he had not sent in any other manner in the marque itself, unless it had been sent before by permission to Soanachilde, or to the aforesaid Gairefred, and he had found it there, and he did not wish to act otherwise than as it pleased the lord the king, or as it had been for a long time in the times of kings. There it was the custom, or the tax collector was granted or confirmed to God himself in his integrity. And while in this case we find that acts or perpetrated in this way, such precepts or confirmations of the previous kings offered us to be relegated, together with many of our faithful: that is, Milo, Helmegand, Hildegar, Chrothard, Drogon, Baugulf, Gislehar, Leuthfred, Raulcon, Theuderic, Maganarius , Nithadus, Waltharius, Wulfarius, and Wicbert, count of our palace, we were seen to have judged, or to have decreed, or to have confirmed, and to have granted anew again, that from this day forth none of the judicial power, neither in the marque itself, nor through their fields, nor the ports , nor of their men, nor of their slaughterers, nor of all the nations whatever come to the aforesaid mark, nor of their towns, nor of the boats, nor of the harbors, nor of the carts, nor of the boats, nor of any toll, nor forager, nor rotatic, nor pontatic, nor portatic, nor salutatic, nor cispitatic, nor mutatic, nor any exact, nor customs, nor those four dinars, of all the nations that come there to the very mark, which Soanachildis and Gairefredus, as we mentioned above, customarily sent to slaying them, neither within the village of Paris, nor in the city itself, from the same place, nor elsewhere who come to the holy festival itself, without any exactness or contrariety, neither you, nor your juniors or successors presuming to exact or exact, unless, as we have said, whatever our treasury might have hoped for from our side, or from all our agents, everything and from all the publican himself to the very house of God should be granted in full, and be pardoned, or vindicated, so that in future times by our authority, or by the authority of former kings let them have it confirmed, or vindicated. Because for

God's sake and for the reverence of the aforesaid saint Dionysius the martyr, or for the remedy of our souls, or for the stability of the kingdom of the Franks, and for our children, or for their posterity, we send this in lights to the very house of St. Dionysius, or to the monks themselves, or to the poor and strangers in our alms. We granted this in all, or confirmed it, so that it would be better for them, for the stability of our kingdom, or for all our troubles, to implore the Lord's mercy more attentively, and that he may advance to the very house of God in increase for eternal and everlasting times. And in order that this confirmation of ours, having been inspected by the very judgment of lord Hildebert, king or of other kings, but also of our uncle Grimoald, the greatest of the house, may be more firmly established, and may be preserved perpetually around the holy house of God, we have decided to sign it with our hand, and to seal it with our ring.

A signal to our lord Peppin, the most glorious king.

I read his order and signed it.

Given what he did on the 10th day of the month Julius, in the second year of our reign, in the name of God successfully.

XV. Peppin's command for the confirmation of the town of Taberniac in the town of Paris (in the year 754).

Peppin, king of the Franks, was a pious man. We believe that we are associated with the eternal Judge in the reward, if we know that he was delegated to the places of the saints, and by our precept signed by the hand of the previous kings with confirmation there, we affirm by our oracle for the love of God and the retribution of the saints. And therefore the venerable man Fulradus, abbot of the special basilica of our patron Saint Dionysius, where the precious martyr himself seems to rest in the body with his associates, or the abbot himself seems to dwell with a large company of monks, or they are known as the military Lord; they suggested to us in a mass petition that some years before the infamous man Guntaldus had delegated or secured a certain village of his called

Taberniacum, situated in the Parisian village, for the remedy of his soul with all his integrity to the very basilica of Lord Dionysius; He held the court itself precariously. In like manner Frodoinus and Geruntus held by the precaria of St. Dionysius, and for the very delegation or confirmation, or the very precarias of the previous king, lord Childebert, and the precaria of our uncle Grimoald the greater house, they offered us to relegate. And since, through the unrighteous greed of evil men, the very town of Taberniacus was abstracted or diminished from the very house of St. Dionysius: the abbot himself, or the congregation itself, requested from the majesty of our kingdom, that we should by our confirmation or deliberation strengthen the commandment, whatever our casindus Teudbertus by our very beneficence He held the town of Tabernia named above, that is, together with the lands, houses, buildings, garrisons, slaves, tenants, inmates, servants, freedmen, servants both of native origin and those transferred from elsewhere, rural and urban, forests and under-vineyards, cultivated and uncultivated lands . those colonies in Acebrelidus and Walion, and that Warinna fiscal through which it is my custom to draw, which Teutbertus held near the town itself, and whatever had been looked upon or possessed for a long time before the town itself; by our authority or confirmation, and for the stability of our kingdom, in the name of God, to the very house of St. Dionysius, often called the town of Taberniacus, with all its integrity or solidity, granted or confirmed; let them have the power to do: and by this authority of ours let the vigor of the one named Fulradus the abbot be confirmed in his right and dominion with God's and our grace on the part of St. Dionysius. And that it should remain unshaken for ages and future times, we decided to confirm it with our hand under it and to seal it with our ring.

The sign of the inglorious lord and most glorious king Peppin.

Widmarus acknowledged the order.

Dated in the third year of our reign, Vermeria in the palace.

16 The decree of King Peppin donating to the monastery of St. Dionysius a castle at the mountain of St. Michael in the village of Virdun (in the year 755).

Peppin, king of the Franks, a pious man. The greatest care and greatest solicitude must be exercised by a prince, so as to skilfully observe those things which have been expounded by the priests of Christ for the expediency of the churches of God, and not to deny them appropriate or convenient benefits, but to procure those things which are for God's purpose to be affected in God's name. Therefore, let him know the sagacity of all the faithful of God and of us, both present and future, because we, for the love of God and Saint Dionysus, our special patron, where Folleradus appears to preside over the abbot and guardian, in the place of Aleco in the village of Veredun, which is called Mount Saint Michael the Archangel, on the river Marsupia (Marsoupe), which Fulfoaldus once gave us for his life, because he wanted to build that castle there to receive our enemies, as has been proved, and for this reason he was sent to the courts to the judgment of the Franks: but Folleradus the abbot or the congregation itself Saint Dionysius begged us for him, and we spared him his life in the love of God and of the Lord Dionysius. Therefore, in our recompense and reparation for the soul of our father Charles, we give the very place and castle to the monastery of the blessed Lord Dionysius, where we were enthroned, with all things belonging to or respecting him, with slaves of both sexes, and also lands, houses, buildings, vineyards, forests, meadows, pastures, waters, watercourses, movable and immovable, or whatever can be said or named, and with the clerics themselves who seem to serve. Therefore, by our present precept, we order and establish that, as it is clear that we have acquired the same place and castle in our palace by the justice and law of the Franks, so in our time and future times the abbot Folleradus himself and his successors, or the holy congregation itself, should hold and let them possess themselves at the holy basilica in perpetuity: and that it may be better for them always to pray for us, or our children, or for the stability of our kingdom and of the Franks, day and night incessantly, or implore the Lord's mercy; and as they promised us, every day they should recite our name both in the masses and in their special prayers at the tomb of St. Dionysius himself: and if we could find an opportunity for them in any other place for this or before, we would willingly grant it to them. And in order that this authority or precept of ours, which they demanded of us, should be successful in regard to the very holy house of God, and that it should continue unshakable or firm for now and in future times, we confirmed it with our own hand below, and ordered it to be sealed with our seal.

A signal to the most glorious lord Peppin the king. He recognized and subscribed to his order.

Given in the fourth of the month of August, in the fourth year of our reign, Compendium in the name of God successfully. Amen.

XVII. Diploma of King Peppin for the monastery of Nantuacensi (in the year 757).

Peppin, king of the Franks, to all our bishops, counts, dukes, abbots, householders, centurions, vicars, and judges, or to all our messengers.

Knowing that we believe that the greatest defense of our kingdom will increase, if we grant [...] appropriate benefits to the places of churches or saints with benevolent deliberation and contribute to the stability of the Lord's protection. Therefore, let your skill know that we, at the request of the venerable man Siagrius, abbot of the monastery of Nantoac, which was built in honor of the blessed Mary, the mother of God, and of Saint Peter the Apostle, or of the rest of the saints, have deemed us to have bestowed such a boon for eternal retribution, that the villages of his monastery, which in modern times or which he seems to have in our office, or in the office of any one, or which divine piety has desired to enlarge in the right of the monastery of the holy place, no public judge shall in any way presume to enter to hear cases from all sides, or to exact restraints. under our dominion. Students, therefore, that neither you, nor our minors or successors, nor any public judicial power in any honor in the towns anywhere in our kingdom, by God's propitiation, to the monastery [...] to enter into hearing disputes, or to demand peace for any reason, nor to remove mansions or sureties without presumption, nor to disturb or condemn them for this; because they serve there from a legitimate calling; or of other servants who seem to serve the monastery itself with a legitimate order, under the fields or boundaries, or borders or over the lands of the aforesaid monastery, which belong to the same legitimate order, the treasury shall not be spared, or from wherever it may hope, from our indulgence, for future safety. in the luminaries of the monastery itself, to the very places of the saints, by our hands, by our authority, may it be accomplished forever; and for the sake of the Lord's name, and for the salvation of our souls, or of our subsequent posterity, we have indulged ourselves with a full gift. Neither the royal sublimity, nor the savage desire of the judges should try to resist. In order that the present authority may continue inviolable both for present and future (times) by the propitiation of God, we have decided to strengthen our hands by the signatures below.

The sign of Peppin, the most glorious king

In the name of God, he wrote Badillo on the tenth day of August in the sixth year of his reign. Act of the Attinian palace in public.

XVIII. The plea of Peppin concerning all the publicans in the market of St. Dionysius who claimed the monastery itself, against Gerardus count of Paris (in the year 758).

Peppin, king of the Franks, an illustrious man. When the agents of St. Dionisio and Follerado, the abbot Aderulf and Rodegarius Compendius, came to the palace on the tenth day of the Month of November, in the eighth year of our reign, where we were to sit to hear the causes of all and to determine the right judgments, where they were seen to have interrupted Count Gerard, because he was remanding and detaining in bad order the toll below Paris from the ships, and the winding and rolling bridges, which from the very day of the mass to Saint Dionysius was always received by the agents of the holy lord Dionysius from ancient times. Wherefore the aforesaid Gerard gave the earl in his answers, that he did not contest the taxman in any other way, except as his predecessors, who had been earls before him, retained the same for his own part. The aforesaid agents of St. Dionysius thus aimed against him and showed the precept of King Dagobert, how he had established the market itself in the village itself, and afterwards when he had delegated and established all the publicans on the part of St. Dionysius. And the lord King Peppin himself affirmed, that ever since his childhood he had seen the same tax collectors having and collecting the parts of St. Dionysius. But Count Gerard would not consent to this in any way, and then they made such a convention that they should once again come together to the legitimate nights in the same palace, and the aforesaid lord Peppin should have defined the very intention, as the law dictated. Finally, the aforesaid messengers and advocates of St. Dionysius, Adrulph and Rotgarius, having come, to the established agreement on the fourth of November, presented such witnesses there, who received the tax collectors themselves into Paris with all their integrity on the side of St. Dionysius. Then they were judged by Widon, Raulcon, Milone, Helmengaud, Rothardo, Gisleharius, or several others, or even Wicbert, count of our palace, as a part of St. Dionysius, or the aforesaid advocates should have confirmed this: which they were seen to have done in the present. For the aforesaid Count Gerard gave such answers as he did not wish to do otherwise, except as the law was, and it pleased the lord the king and his faithful who dwelt there. Wherefore also Gerard himself said before them that he was going out from among the aforesaid tax collectors. Wherefore at that time it was expedient and necessary for them, that they should have received such notice of this fact, that from this time and day the part of St. Dionysius, or his agents, would be able to reside safely and quietly among them, so that there might be between them at all times a quiet and sudden cause.

A sign + to the most glorious lord Peppin the king.

He recognized his order and signed it.

Given on the third day of November, in the year above written, in the name of God.

XIX. Diploma of Peppin, king of the Franks, by which he confirms the possessions of the monastery of Honaugi. Given on December 15, 759.

Peppin, king of the Franks, an illustrious man. To all the bishops, abbots, dukes, counts, domestics, vicars, centenarians, and all our missionaries, both present and future. Knowing that we believe that the most important fortification of our kingdom will increase, if we grant convenient benefits to the places of the churches with benevolent deliberation, we trust that the Lord will continue stably under his protection. Therefore, let your wisdom know that we, at the request of the venerable man Bishop Dubani, have been granted such a favor for eternal retribution, as to the villages or property of the church of St. Michael the Archangel from the monastery which was built on the island of the Rhine called Hohenaugia, or who seems to have the office of any one, or whom divine piety wills to enlarge in the right of the holy place itself, no public judge presumes to enter in to hear cases, or to demand restraints from all sides, but the aforesaid Dubanus, or his successors for the sake of the name of the Lord or of St. Michael under in the name of immunity he should be able to dominate the very things. Therefore we preemptively command that neither you, nor your juniors, nor your successors, nor any public judicial power, at any time in any place in our kingdom, shall be bestowed by the church, or royal, or by the generosity of private persons, or good men, or that they have formerly been God-fearing. . but whatever thence for those who serve, who are under the fields or vineyards, or over the lands of the aforesaid church of St. Michael, commanding, or who command anywhere; and there they seem to look in a legitimate order, that our treasury, either from the friars, or from wherever we may hope from our indulgence, for the future safety of the lights of the church itself, may proceed forever through the hands of their agents to the church itself; and that for the sake of the Lord's name and the remedy for our souls, or our subsequent posterity, we have indulged with full devotion, and neither royal sublimity, nor the belated cupidity of any judge shall attempt to resist. And in order that the present authority may continue both in present and future times, by the help of God, we have decided to affirm it with our hand under it, or to seal it with our ring.

The sign of Peppin the most glorious king.

In the name of God, Baddilo, he recognized and wrote.

Given on the fifteenth of September, in the seventh year of the reign of King Peppin. Act Duria, in the name of God successfully. Amen.

XX. Diploma of king Peppin confirming the goods and rights of the abbey of Murbac (year 760).

Pepin, the illustrious king of the Franks. It behooves the chief clemency of the congregations to lend a kind ear, and especially for the saving of souls from our previous kings and predecessors we prove that they were pardoned to the places of the churches, we must consider with a devout mind and not deny the appropriate benefits that we deserve to be partakers of the reward but confirm with the most robust right for our oracles. Therefore, by the gift of God, the venerable man Baldobert, abbot of the monastery of Vivario Pilgrims, which is situated in the village of Alsace above the river Morbach, which was built in honor of St. by the fact that our ancestors once, through their authorities, signed with their hands the estates of the church itself, which it possessed at the present time, as much from the gifts of the princes or of Eberhard, who founded the monastery itself with his alms, as from the generosity of the peasants, or that the whole estate had previously been delegated to God-fearing men granted immunity, that no public judge should enter into the towns or property of his own church, either to hear cases, or to demand reliefs, or to make mansions or make ready, or to remove sureties, or to separate the people of the church itself from any causes, nor to demand any redistribution there; hence and the precept already mentioned by our predecessors, or by their confirmation, the aforesaid abbot Baldobert, the rector of the monastery, shows us to rebind for the same benefit about the same or mentioned church which he claims to have been preserved until now. But instead of affirming his interest, he asked our highness to confirm this once again about the monastery itself, or about the monks themselves, our authority in general. Whose petition for the reverence of the place itself, that we may deserve to be associated with the reward, we were seen with the fullest willingness to have lent or confirmed in all things. Therefore, we preemptively order that no public judge should be involved in the affairs or resources of the church itself, neither to hear cases, nor to demand reliefs, nor to make mansions or make ready, nor to take away sureties, nor his men so naive as slaves who seem to command over their lands or miti, who they see there that they should not be separated from any causes, nor should they enter there without requiring any redistribution; ours was able to rule in the lights of Lord Leodegarius himself and of St. Peter and St. Mary for the stability of our kingdom forever. And in order that this authority may be evident both in present and future times, we have confirmed it under our hand and ordered it to be sealed with our ring.

XXI. The diploma of Peppin, king of the Franks, for the monastery of Honaugie, given in verse 760.

Peppin, king of the Franks, an illustrious man, to the holy and apostolic lords and venerable Fathers in Christ, to all the bishops, abbots, or illustrious and magnificent men, leaders, counts, domestics, vicars, centurions, and all agents. We think that it is right that the requests of the priests, which pertain to the departure for the holy places, should be brought to fruition, by the presbytery of Christ. Therefore in Christ Father Dubanus, the bishop or abbot of the monastery of Hohenaugia in the village of Alsace, on the river Rhine, which was built in honor of St. Michael and St. Peter and St. Paul, or the rest of the saints, gloriously asked the majesty of our kingdom, so that while the monastery itself was about the contribution of our ancestors, or it seems to have been built by the auxiliaries of God-fearing men, we have the whole body of its resources, both because the predecessors of the abbots worked there, as well as because Dubanus himself seems to have increased or procured from the things of the monastery, which are known to have been there, and that from the holy place itself modern possessed at the time, we ought by ours to confirm in general the precept that your greatness does not doubt that you have lent us for divine respect or for the increase of our reward; and also the privilege of the monastery itself, which according to the institution of the ancient Fathers and the rest of the bishops they were seen to have earned, and which it is known to have been outlined by our authority, or by the laws of the rest of the successors of our ancestors, according to which before it was fortified by our previous precept of forbidding them, for perpetual We decided to strengthen stability. Therefore, we preemptively order that all the resources of the monastery, whatever has been legally acquired or procured either by royal contribution, or by the function of private persons, or by the predecessors of the abbots, or by the Bishop of Dubano or the abbot, nay, whatever has been properly acquired, whatever the dominion of the holy monastery itself Wheresoever in modern times the Hohenaugiensis is seen to possess villages, houses, manors, vineyards, forests, meadows, pastures, or any benefices, with the order of the cavalry, supported by this authority without any unlawful controversies there, both in the present and in the future time, may Christ the Archangel prosper in increase. And whence the monastery itself had until now been granted and up to now preserved, or strengthened around it by our predecessors' kings, thus and previously having been cut off from any superfluous restlessness of yours, may that order be able in our speech, with the help of the Lord, to continue throughout time, both you and your successors. where there is necessity in the conditions of the monastery itself, you should do just to impart help; so that it would be better for the assembly of the monastery itself to constantly invoke the Lord's mercy for our safety or the stability of our kingdom. And in order that this precept may subsist in firm stability, we have decided to strengthen it below with our own hand, and to seal it with our ring.

The sign of the most glorious lord Peppin the king.

Wulmarus recognized the order and wrote.

XXII. Peppin, king to Giomadus, the archbishop, and of the church of Treviso, confirms the churches of Sts. Maximinus, Paulinus, Eucharius, and Oreum, St. Martin, and whatever the church of Trier has and will have on this side of the Rhine and the Liger, and that it be free from tolls (in 761).

In the name of the Lord God eternal and our Savior Jesus Christ. Peppin, by divine providence, king of the Franks. If, by our liberality, we bestow some benefit upon the places dedicated to God and relieve the ecclesiastical needs of our priests by means of assistance, and protect ourselves with royal protection, we believe that this will be of definite benefit to us both in passing over the temporal and mortal life, and in obtaining eternal happiness. Accordingly, let him know the sagacity of all our faithful, both present and future, because the venerable man Giomadus, archbishop of the holy church of Trier, presented to our obstinacy the commandment of the former kings of the Franks, in which it was inserted that our predecessors, that is, the Franks, all things, whatever good and holy men for divine contemplation with a view to the part of the church of St. Peter of Trier, they relegated them to the church of Trier, confirmed them with the authorities of their people, in so far as their kingdom was protected by heavenly help, and afterwards they should reign with Christ, King of kings, in heaven. For the firmness of the matter, the same aforesaid prince Giomadus requested our highness, that following the manner of our fathers, or of the predecessors of the kings, we should order this order of our authority, for the love of God and the reverence of St. Peter, to be done concerning the same things; to whose request we willingly consented, and we decreed that this precept of our authority towards the church itself, for the love of divine worship, and for the remedy of our souls, should be done, by which we command and order that all the facilities or things belonging to the church of St. Peter of Treverice, namely, the cell of St. Maximinus, which was built in the territory of St. Peter, the prince of the apostles, and the churches of St. Paulinus and St. Eucharius, and the monastery of St. Mary, which Lord Modoaltus, the priest, built from the foundation of the same church in the territory of St. Peter, which is called Orca, and the church of St. Martin built in the village of Ambitivo. and the rest of the basilicas, castles, villages, towns, vineyards, forests, people, and whatever God has given to the same church in future growth on this side of the Rhine and Liger rivers, standing in our kingdom, all under the right and power of the church of St. Peter of Trier and its priest in perpetual possession let them continue Moreover, we decree in the same way that none of the public judges, or anyone from the judicial power in monasteries, churches, castles, villages or fields, or the rest of the possessions of the aforesaid church, as well as beyond the Rhine or Liger rivers, in villages or territories, under the power of the kingdom of ours, the aforesaid church owns it, or that thereafter in the right of the holy place itself divine piety wills to be increased, to hear cases, or to demand reliefs or tributes, or to exact certain exiles, or to make mansions or parratas, or to remove sureties, or to separate men from the church itself, nor They do not at all presume to demand unjust exactions, or exact tolls, in our and future times, or to exact those things which have been mentioned above; but let the aforesaid prince and his successors possess all the aforesaid monasteries, villages, villages, and forts with their adjacencies, whole forever, for the remedy of our souls or of our parents, in quiet order, and to faithfully obey our command, and for the safety of our spouses and children , or even of the whole kingdom, given to us by God, and preserved by his most merciful mercy, together with the clergy and the people subject to him, to constantly implore immense mercy. And whatever of the aforesaid matters the right of the church could demand from the treasury, we granted the same to the church in its entirety, that is to say, that it may be continually increased and supplemented to perform the service of God. Therefore, this authority of ours, that it may obtain fuller vigor in the name of God, and be believed more truly by the faithful of God's holy church, and that is to say, in our present and future times, and be more diligently preserved by our successors, we have confirmed it with our own hand below, and ordered it to be sealed with the impression of our ring .

The sign of Peppin, the most successful king. I, Joseph the subdeacon, recognized Wulfart in turn. Given on the 15th day of July, indictment 13, in the ninth year of the reign of the illustrious king.

Act Tulpiacko in the name of God successfully, amen.

XXIII. Diploma of king Peppin, in which he gives the town of Tinningen to the church of Fulda (in 762).

Peppin, king of the Franks, was a illustrious man. As the Apostle says, we have brought nothing into this world, and there is no doubt that we shall be able to take nothing out of it with us, except that for the sake of the salvation of the soul, with a devoted mind, we are seen to spread in the holy places, inspiring God. with eternal recompense we give from the present day to the monastery of Fulda, which was built in honor of the holy Savior, which Saint Boniface built with a new work, where the precious martyr himself rests in body, but rather with the most prompt devotion we hand over the town called Thininga, situated in the village of Rezi on the river called Act with all integrity, whatever appears to look upon or belong to the town itself, that is to say, both the lands, the manors, the manors, the woods, the marks or borders, the fields, the meadows, the pastures, the waters, or the streams, the movable and immovable governors, the whole and to the whole, as we have said, from the present day to the very monastery of St. Salvator where the precious martyr St. Boniface himself rests in body, on the river Fulda, through this series of tradition for the increase of our wages we give perpetually to possess, so that from and that day the directors of the monastery itself, itself the town called Tininga, with all its adjacencies or appendages, for the advancement of the Church itself, let them hold and possess it, and let it continue to increase for them forever; and in order that this authority may be more firmly established, or be better preserved for many times, we have secured it under it, or sealed it with our ring.

A sign to Peppin the most glorious king.

Hitherius in the turn of Baddillon, given in the month of June, in the ninth year of our reign. Act of Atiniago in the public palace.

XXIV. The testament of Saint Salvator, which Peppin ordered to be made king in the abbey of Prumien (in the year 762).

Pepin, king of the Franks, a man of renown. Because it is clear that divine providence has brought us to the throne of the kingdom, it is necessary to exercise those things in the name of God, in which we are able to obtain rather the grace and will of the Most High. For we remember the Gospel itself, in which it says: He who does the will of my Father, who is in heaven, will himself enter the kingdom of heaven. And because kings rule from God, he has committed nations and kingdoms to us out of his mercy to govern, to provide that we may be exalted rulers of the poor, and not neglect to rule and educate the poor for the love of Christ. Indeed, God commanded Moses the lawgiver to arrange the tabernacle of mercy; We know that Solomon and every king adorned the temple built in his name with gold and stones. For we, although we are not so great as to be able to equalize with them, nevertheless, what we can more easily, from our own resources which we have, cooperating with the Lord, we desire to offer the same to him, because, as the Apostle says, we have brought nothing into this world, nor because we will be able to bring anything out of it, but we believe that it is conducive to the salvation of the soul, whatever we seem to distribute to the Lord with a devout mind about transitory things. Therefore, while it is known to all, both relatives and foreign nations, we and our spouse Bertrada in the love of Saint Savior, and also of Saint Mary, mother of God, and of the blessed princes of the apostles Peter and Paul, or of Saint John the Baptist, or of the martyrs of Saint Stephen, Dionysius and Mauritius, and the confessors Martin, Vedast, and Germani, to build a monastery on our property, which is situated below the borders of Baden and Ardennes, where the stream called Berdenbach enters Prumia, in the very monastery of the church of the sandals of our Lord Jesus Christ, nor We were seen to store the remains of the mother Mary himself, and of the other saints, of whom we have already made mention above, and there we appointed monks, who were under the rule of holy conduct, or according to the preceding Fathers. . . should be exercised at all, to the extent that those who are called solitary monks are able to rejoice in perfect rest under the guidance of the Lord throughout the ages, and living under the holy rule and following the life of the blessed Fathers for the state of the Church and the longevity of our kingdom, and not only as our wife and children and the Catholic people, Christ's apostles ought more fully to invoke the Lord's mercy. However, it must be provided that while it is established by us for the love of Christ that the monastery itself has been founded by a new work, how shall we go about it, how in future the priests and monks who will be there should live or have comfort and tranquility, and by no means should the shepherd find the scattered sheep, who will find the flock He has committed his providence to us, but those who are qualified may at the same time give praises to Almighty God day and night. For this reason, by divine grace inspiring us, I and my wife Bertrada give to the very most sacred place, which we built in honor of St. Savior or St. Mary, our property in the village of Charos, a town called Rumeresheim, as well as that portion which came to me from my father Charles, and that portion of Bertrada himself, which his father Herebert left to him in dowry, together with the appendages, or with all his integrity, except for some vassals of these names: Wucdramno, Arnulfo, Crodoaldo, Wanulfo, Ghiorino, Chrodramno, Wulfrido, Tancrado, Adalberto, Beringhiso., Zebelinde. We therefore retain these slaves for our work, but in the rest we hand over and transfer the town itself with all its integrity to the very holy place, on the border of which the very monastery of St. Salvator was founded, and that mansion above Prumia, where the stream called Escutmisbach flows into Prumia, which was built on the border of the aforesaid town. In the same way we give to the aforesaid monastery in the village of Muslinse, on the river Moselle, our villages by the names of Meringum (Mering), Scoacum (Schweich), together with their merit and boundaries or appendages. We also give our village in the village of Biden, which is called Marciaco (Mertich), together with its merits and appendages. In the same way we give to the monastery itself our villa in the village of Effinse Sarabodis (Sarensdorf) together with its solidity, borders and appendages, as it was owned by Garabert. We deliver two other places in Carasco to the same monastery of Wathit-Lendorp and Birgisburias with all their adjacencies and appendages. In the same way we give in the village of Riboariens that portion in Reginbach (Reinbach), which our vassal Aglibertus had by benefice and my father Charles left to me as a dowry, and that other portion in the village itself, which Herbert left to my wife Bertrada as a dowry. We also confirm there and those things which were previously delegated to the church itself by instruments of paper there, with all their integrity. We therefore hand over to the very most sacred place the above-comprehended cell, by right of our property, in the village of Spire, which was built in honor of St. Medard, with its villages and appendages, which Herlibandus and Weolentius, as well as Bagulfus, handed over to me, whole and in their entirety, as well as the ministries of the church. and other matters pertaining thereto. We also give to the monastery itself another cell, which is called Casleoca, which is situated below the borders of Senciaco, and was built in honor of Saint Peter, with all its adjacencies or appendages. We therefore also confirm the third cell to the holy place itself, which is called Ruivinio in the village of Lomen on the river Meuse, which was built in honor of Saint Mary, with all its merits and appendages. On that condition we confirm the above-mentioned things, both the villages and the cells, with all their integrity to the monastery itself, that is, together with the lands, houses, buildings, acropolis, mancipi, vineyards, forests, fields, meadows, pastures, waters, waters with streams, movable and immovable, money, savings of both sexes, flocks with shepherds, everything and from everything, from the present day and thereafter, without any hindrance, at all times the aforesaid things to the monastery of Saint Salvator, which has already been mentioned many times, proceed in increments. However, we wish that the monastery of Saint Savior itself, or the things that belong to the monastery itself, both those which have been confirmed by our authority, and those which have previously been contributed by those who fear God, should be in our power or defense or of our heirs, and the assembly itself, which We admitted into the monastery itself, or an abbot named Assuerus, or his successors, as long as he wished to fight there under the holy rule with the help of God. We do not admit an abbot or a monk from another congregation against our order, nor our heirs. And because we want the monastery itself to be safe from all care of the seculars, it is necessary that the provision of our clemency should provide for the future rest of the brothers who remain there by a healthy ordination, in so far as they continue in the service of God by supporting his grace. We also grant you, by our authority, that from the congregation of Lord Romanus and Wolfranus the bishops, whom we gathered in this convent of St. Salvator, when the abbot departed from this life, together with our consent and yours, you must regularly elect an abbot from the congregation itself. And that you, for the remedy of our souls and of our spouses and children and of our heirs, and for the stability of the whole empire granted to us by God, and for the preservation of his gratuitous mercy for eternity, may be pleased to continually implore the mercy of our Lord our Savior Jesus Christ, and to persevere in his praises day and night, and removed from temporal meditations, and intent on the contemplation of heavenly joys with a free mind, we order that no prejudices and grievances be brought upon us by any of the bishops or laymen, and our heirs by no arts, while the monks themselves seem to behave regularly and faithfully on our side or our heirs, our heirs let them protect themselves in our convent, as they have been seen. By the authority of God, we have established the place itself, so that it may remain unshaken for eternity, for the growth of our souls, or of our heirs. And in order that our authority might be more firmly established, or better preserved for ever, we resolved to strengthen it with our own hand. I Pipinus and my wife Bertrada.

The sign + of Charles my son consenting.

Sign + Charles's sons agree	Bishop Wiemadi
Bishop Genebaud.	Bishop Drocon.
Bishop Gaurleni.	Bishop Theodard
Bishop Fulcarius.	Warini.
Bishop Adelfred	Welanti.
Bishop Wulfranni	Bangulf
Bishop Megingaudi	Gerhard
Bishop Bertelin.	Troanie.
Bishop Basini	Walter.

Herloin.   Count Gumbert
Warini.

In the name of God Bradilo [Baddilo] recognized and signed. Dated in the month of August, on the 13th day, in the 11th year of the reign of Pepin the glorious king. Act of Trisgodros town state in the name of God successfully, amen.

XXV. King Peppin's diploma for the construction and endowment of the monastery of Prumi (in 762).

Peppin, king of the Franks, an illustrious man. Since it is clear that divine providence has anointed us in the kingdom of the throne, it is necessary to exercise them in the name of God, in which we can rather achieve the grace and will of the Most High. For we remember the gospel itself, in which he says: He who does the will of my Father who is in heaven will himself enter the kingdom of heaven. And because kings rule by God, he has entrusted nations and kingdoms to us for his mercy, to see that we are also exalted rulers in riches, and do not neglect to govern and educate the poor for the love of Christ. God indeed commanded Moses the lawgiver to adorn the tabernacle of mercy; We also know that King Solomon decorated the temple built in his name with gold and stones. For we, although we are not so great as to be able to equalize with them, yet what we can more easily, from our own resources, we desire to offer to the Lord, cooperating with him, because, as the Apostle says, we have brought nothing into this world, and no doubt, because we have nothing to offer from it we shall be able to do so: but we believe that this will only advance the salvation of the soul, whatever we seem to distribute to the Lord with a devout mind about transitory things. Therefore, while it is known to all, both relatives and foreign nations, we and our spouse Bertrada in the love of the holy Savior, as well as the holy Mother of God Mary, and the blessed princes of the apostles Peter and Paul, or Saint John the Baptist, or also the martyrs Saints Stephen, Dionysius and Maurice, and the confessors Martin, Vedast, and Germani, to build a monastery on our property, which is situated below the borders of Biddense (Bidburg) and Arduenne, where the stream called Berdenbach enters Prumia. In the church of the monastery itself, we were seen to store the relics of the sandals of our Lord Jesus Christ, as well as of his mother Mary, and of the other saints, of whom we have already made mention above, and there we appointed monks who should be exercised entirely under the norm of holy behavior, or according to the previous fathers. inasmuch as those who are called solitary monks may be able to exult in perfect rest in the Lord as their guide throughout the ages, and living under the holy rule, and following the life of the blessed Fathers, for the state of the Church and the longevity of our kingdom, as well as for our wife and children, and for the Catholic people, they should owe more fully to Christ the Archangel to invoke the mercy of the Lord. However, it must be provided that while it is established by us for the love of Christ that the monastery itself has been founded by a new work, how shall we proceed, how shall the priests and monks who are present there live, and have comfort and tranquility, and by no means find a shepherd with scattered sheep, who will find the flock He committed his providence to us, but those who were qualified at the same time could sing praises to Almighty God long and night. For this reason, with divine grace inspiring us, I and my wife Bertrada give to the very most sacred place, which we built in honor of St. Savior or St. Mary, the things of our property in the village of Chorosvilla, which is called Rumeresheim, as well as that portion that belonged to my father Charles It came to me, as well as that portion of Bertrada herself, which her father Herbert left her in dowry, with the appendages, with all her integrity, except for some servants. We therefore retain these slaves for our work, but in the rest, we hand over and transfer the town itself with all its integrity to the very holy place, on the border of which the very monastery of St. Savior was founded; and that mansion above Prumia, where the stream called Escutmisbach flows into Prumia, which was built on the border of the aforesaid town. In the same way we give to the aforesaid monastery in the village of Muslinse on the river Moselle our villages by these names, Meringum (Mering) and Sacocum (Schivach), together with their merits and boundaries or appendages. We give also our town of Bedense, which is called Marciaco (Merthscb), together with its merits and appendages. In the same way we give to the monastery itself our villa in the village of Eiflin, the villa of Sarabodis (Sarensdorff), together with its solidity, boundaries and appendages, as it was possessed by Garabert. We deliver two other places in Carasius to the same monastery of Wathitlindorff and Birgisburias with all their adjacencies and appendages. In the same way we give in the village of Biboarien that portion in Reginbach (Rheimbach), which our vassal Aglibertus had by virtue of a benefice, and which my father Charles left to me in inheritance; and that other portion in the town itself, which Herbert left to my wife Bertrada in inheritance. We also confirm there and those matters which were previously delegated to the church itself by means of charters there, with all their integrity. Therefore, we hand over to the very most sacred place the above-comprehended cell by right of our property in a place called Altrepio, on the river Rhine, in the village of Spire, which was built in honor of St. Medard, with its villages and appendages, which Herlibandus and Wiolentius, as well as Bagulfus, handed over to me. We also give to the monastery itself another cell, which is called Gasteaco, which is situated below the boundaries of Senciaco, and was built in honor of St. Peter, with all its adjacencies or appendages. We therefore also confirm the third cell to the holy place itself, which is called Ruivinio, in the village of Lomen on the river Meuse, which was built in honor of Saint Mary, with all its merits and appendages. On the said condition, we confirm the things above written, both the villages and the cells, with all their integrity to the monastery itself, that is, together with the lands, houses, buildings, acrolas, mancipes, vineyards, woods, fields, meadows, pastures, waters, and waters with streams, movable and immovable, money, savings of both sexes, flocks with shepherds, everything and from everything from the present day onwards, without any hindrance, at all times the aforesaid things to the monastery of the holy Savior, as has already been said many times, may proceed in increments; that the monastery of the holy Savior itself, or the things which pertain to the monastery itself, such as have been confirmed by our authority, and have been previously contributed by those who fear God, may be in our power, or defense, or that of our heirs; and the congregation itself, which we admitted into the monastery itself, or the abbot named Assuerus, and the successors of the same, while under the holy rule they wished to fight there with the help of God, we did not interrupt from another congregation there an abbot, nor a monk against our order, nor our heirs. And because we want the monastery itself to be safe from all secular care, it is necessary that the provision of our clemency should provide for the future rest of the brothers who remain there by a healthy arrangement. in so far as they continue in the service of God, supported by his grace. We also grant you, by our authority, that from the congregation of Lord Roman and Wolfran, the bishops whom we gathered in this convent of Saint Salvator, when the abbot departed from this life, together with our consent and yours, you must regularly elect an abbot from the congregation itself. And that you, for the remedy of our souls, and of our spouses, and of our children, and of our heirs, and for the stability of the whole empire granted to us by God, and his gratuitous mercy to be preserved to eternity, may delight to implore the mercy of our Lord Jesus Christ continually, and in his praises day and night to tighten and, removed from temporal meditations, we command to concentrate with a free mind on the contemplation of the heavenly joys, so that no prejudices and grievances may be inflicted by any of the bishops or laymen, and our heirs by any arts, while the monks themselves seem to conduct themselves regularly and faithfully on our side, or on the part of our heirs, the heirs let ours protect themselves in this convent of ours, as they have been seen, we have established the place itself by God, so that the place may remain unshaken for ever and ever for the growth of our souls or our heirs. And in order that this authority of ours may be firmly held, and better preserved for ever, we have resolved to strengthen it with our own hand.

I, Peppin, and my wife, Bertrada.

Sig. Charles, the son of the consenting	*Sig. + Count Drocon*
	Sig. + Count Theodard
Sig. + Charles's sons will agree.	*Sig. + Count Warin.*
Sig. + bishop of Genebaud	*Sig. + Count Welanti*
Sig. + bishop of Gaul	*Sig. + Count Gangulf.*
Sig. + Bishop Fulcaricus	*Sig. + Count Gerhard*
Sig. + Bishop Adelfred	*Sig. + Froamed. count*
Sig. + Bishop of Wulfran.	*Sig. Count Waltharius.*
Sig. + Bishop of Megingaud.	*Sig. + Count of Horloin Sig. +*
Sig. + the bishop of Berthelin.	*Count Humbert*
Sig. + Bishop of Basin.	*Sig. + Count Raculfi*
Sig. + Bishop Wiomadi	*Sig. + Count Warin.*

In the name of God Bradilo recognized and signed. Acted in the month of August, on the 13th, in the year 11, in the reign of Peppin the glorious king.

Actus Trisgodios town state successfully in the name of God. Amen.

XXVI. Diploma by which King Peppin confirms all his possessions in the monastery of Honaugie.

Peppin, king of the Franks, an illustrious man, to the holy and apostolic lords and venerable fathers in Christ, to all the bishops, abbots, or illustrious and magnificent men, leaders, counts, domestics, vicars, centurions, and all agents.

We think it is right that the requests of the priests, which pertain to the progress of the holy places, should be brought to fruition before Christ. Therefore in Christ Father Dubanus, the bishop or abbot of the monastery of Hohenaugia in the village of Alsace on the river Rhine, which was built in honor of St. Michael and St. Peter and St. Paul or the rest of the saints, asked the majesty of our glorious kingdom, so that while the monastery itself was about the contribution of our ancestors, or the helper seems to have been built of men who fear God, we have the whole body of his faculties, both because the predecessors of the abbots worked there, and because Dubanus himself seems to have increased, or procured from the things of the monastery, which are known to have been there, and that from the holy place itself in modern times possessed at the time, we should generally confirm the precept, which your greatness has no doubt provided for us for divine respect or for the increase of our reward; and also the privilege of the monastery itself, which according to the institution of the ancient Fathers and the rest of the bishops they were seen to have earned, and which is known to have been outlined by our authority, or that of the rest of the successors of the kings of our ancestors, according to which before it was fortified by our previous precept of forbidding them, for perpetual We decided to strengthen stability. Therefore we command those in command that all the resources of the monastery itself, whatever, either by royal contribution, or by the office of private individuals, or by the predecessors of the abbots, or by Bishop Dubano or the abbot, has been lawfully acquired or procured there; at the time of the farms, houses, manors, vineyards, woods, meadows, pastures, or of any benefice he is seen to possess with the order of equity, supported by this authority without any illegal controversies therein, both in the present and in the future time, let Christ the Archangel prosper in increase. And wherever the monastery itself has until now been granted and until now preserved, or strengthened around it by our predecessors' kings, so and before, cut off from any unnecessary disturbances, may that order be able to continue in our word, helping the Lord throughout the ages, and you and your successors. where there is a need in the conditions of the monastery itself, do just cause to impart help; so that it would be better for the assembly of the monastery itself to constantly invoke the Lord's mercy for our safety or the stability of our kingdom. And in order that this precept may stand in firm stability, we have decided to strengthen it with our own hand below and to seal it with our ring.

The sign + of the most glorious lord Peppin the king.

Wulmarus recognized the order and wrote.

XXVII. Immunity granted to the abbey of Prumien by King Peppin (in 763).

Peppin, king of the Franks, a man of renown, to all the bishops, abbots, dukes, counts, domestics, vicars, centurions, or all our messengers. We believe that the greatest strength of our kingdom will increase, if we grant the benefits to the appropriate places of the saints, or to the churches, by benevolent deliberation, and trusting to the Lord's protection, and to continue stably.

Let your skill, therefore, know how we were seen to have indulged in the monastery called Prumia, which we built in honor of the holy Savior, from a new work, where Assuerus the abbot seems to be presiding. in our time, or in the office of any one he seems to have, or which afterwards in the right of the monastery itself, and the divine mercy will extend to its rulers, no public judge, without the judgment of us, or of our heirs, either by hearing cases, or demanding restraints from all sides, at any time not he presumes to enter: but we have granted this to the monastery itself and to its governors. And under the name of immunity, under the protection or defense of us or our heirs, they should rest quietly in the Lord.

We decree, therefore, that neither you, nor your juniors, nor your successors, nor any public judicial power, shall at any time, at any time, enter into the villages, wherever in our realms of the monastery of Prumi, either royally or by the generosity of private individuals, or who have previously been in propitiation to Christ, to to enter into the hearing of disputes, or to demand peace for any reason, nor to remove apartments or ready ones, or to remove sureties without presuming to do so; but whatever from thenceforth, either to servants or to ecclesiastical men, who are below the fields, or borders, or commanding above the ground of the aforesaid monastery, the treasury, or from the freed, or from wherever he could hope, from our indulgence for the future safety in the lights of the above-mentioned monastery itself, through the hands of their agents for ever, and that for the sake of the Lord's name, and the remedy of our souls, or of our subsequent posterity, we have indulged ourselves with full devotion to the monastery in honor of the holy Saviour, and neither the royal sublimity, nor the savage greed of any judge shall attempt to resist.

And in order that this authority may continue inviolate both for present and future times, God helper, we have decided to strengthen our hands with our signatures below and have ordered to seal them with our ring.

The sign of the lord of the most glorious king Peppin. In the name of God, Bernericus, in the place of Baddillon, acknowledged it, and signed it.

Given on the third day of the Ninth of Augustus, in the twelfth year of the reign of our lord Pepin.

Act of the public palace of Massarius. In the name of God, happily. Amen.

ROYAL FRANKISH DIPLOMAS

XXVIII. The testament of Heddon, bishop of Argentina, or the charter of the foundation and donation of the monastery of Ettenheim, on March 13, 763.

In the name of the Father, and of the Son, and of the Holy Spirit. I, in the name of God, Eddo Peccator, called the bishop of the city of Argentina, while it was known to me how our predecessor, Lord Wicgerinus, the bishop, built a monastery in the Black Forest, in Marche Etinheim, in a place called Monks' Cells above the river Undussa, of his new work in honor of Saint Mary of the ever-virgin, and of St. John the Baptist, and of St. Peter the Apostle, and of the rest of the saints, and had gathered the monks there, and had given to that place something of the things of St. Mary; and we later found the monastery itself abandoned by the negligence of our ancestors. Therefore, it pleased us, by the provision of our Lord Peppin, the glorious king, that I should gather monks there, who should live according to the rule of St. Benedict: which I did so and appointed there a most reverend man named Hildolf as abbot. We also gave to the monastery itself, with the consent of the glorious king Peppin, and of the brothers, or of our citizens living in the episcopate, for the stipend of the monks themselves, whatever we had acquired from Ernest the Duke in the lands named in the village of Brisgaven, that is to say, the estate which Ernest himself had in the town called Forcheim, or in Baldingen, and in Roswilare, and in Wellengen, and in Riegola, or whatever Ernnust himself was seen to possess in Alamania, or in Mordunouwa. Moreover, and concerning the affairs of St. Mary, we granted to the same brothers serving God there, with the permission of the aforesaid King Peppin, and with the consent of all those who live in the episcopate, the town of Endingen, with all that seems to belong to our treasury, and in Burcheim, and in Gruningen, or in Mordunowa, in the town which is called Chipinheim, and in Schopfheim, or in Mutherisheim, whatever we acquired there. For this we also granted to the same monks in a town called Rustum, situated on the bank of the Rhine, power below the rivers Rhine and Helzaha, to make meadows, ponds, and mills, to conduct fishing with our fishermen, and also to catch fish with the sable, in all halves. We also gave in the town itself our servant named Thuhari, with his wife named Eberhilde, and his children and all his belongings to the aforesaid cell for perpetual service; and shortly one in our city Strassburg, with the slaves whom Thengarius had acquired there and had for our benefit, and outside the city one rise which Magilindis had with her daughter Ercalinde, and in the town of Hugesperga one residence at the Hospital. Basilicas also which seemed to belong to our right, namely; one in Etenheim in honor of Saint Mary, and another in Rustum, the aforesaid town in honor of Saint Peter the Apostle, and on the other side of the Rhine in the town called Hepheka in honor of the blessed Mary, and in Beneveldim the basilica of Saints Sixtus and Lawrence, with two hubs, and We granted all the tithes of those things which seem to be subject to them, for the payment of the monks themselves, so that they may have free power over them for their benefit. We also gave in the town of Rubiacus two hubas with their houses, vineyards, and the servants below written, to Wolfger, Gantzfrid, Udalharius with his wife and his children, Landulf, and Fanagulf, and Blidulf with their children, and in the town of Marsalla half a pan of salt to the aforesaid cell in the pay of the monks themselves. In the region of Argouwe also all the churches and all the tithes, namely in Spietz, and in Scartilinga, or in Biberussa, and in the other places which are subjacent to our dominion, and all the censuses which we have hitherto had of that land in our power, due to the same monastery, and to the monks themselves the honor of our Lord Jesus Christ and of his most pious mother Mary the perpetual virgin, and of Saint John the Baptist, and of the holy apostles Peter and Paul, and of all the Saints, whose memory is celebrated there every day, for the increase of the reward of eternal life, or for the peace of the province we have given and consigned, so that From then on, whatever they want to do for the benefit of the monastery or themselves, they have free and firm power to have, to hold, to give, to do. Now these aforesaid things and places, which we consigned to the aforesaid cell, and which, by the help of God, we were still able to acquire for the same cell, with the counsel of the aforesaid glorious king Peppin, and the consent of all his friends and princes, we established and deemed by perpetual law to be quite sufficient for the daily stipend to the thirty brothers and to those who serve them daily, as leading a cenobial life, and obeying the rules of St. Benedict in all things, for the safety and prosperity of the kings, and also for the stability of Christianity, and their religion always does not cease to lament before God. But if any one, which I do not believe to be done, such as myself or any of my successors, or any one contrary to this testament, which I in good faith asked to be made or written, should come, or wish to break it, especially if he refuses to amend himself for this cause, let him fear the wrath of God and the offense of St. Mary and St. Peter the Apostle, and of all the saints, and the punishments of hell, and in addition he shall pay ten pounds of gold and thirty pounds of silver to that monastery, and what he repeats, nothing shall be worth claiming. And that this letter, or this testament, may continue to be sound at all times, I beseech and offer with a humble prayer, that my successors may be worthy to preserve our deeds, for the increase of eternal retribution, which have been confirmed by royal authority, uncorrupted, if they also wish that their deeds should remain preserved. , based on the stipulation. This testament was made in the city of Argentina on the third day of March, in the eleventh year of the reign of our Lord Peppin the glorious King, and of Eddon the venerable bishop. I, in the name of God, Eddo the sinner, by the mercy of the devoted bishop, read and signed this testament made by me.

The sign + of the Count of Chrodard. In the name of Christ,

> *I, Remedius, a sinner and bishop, read the deeds of my former bishop, Eddon, and agreed and signed them.*

I, Einhard, wrote and signed the widely requested

XXIX. Egidius, an illustrious man, became a monk at the monastery of Prumien and made a notable donation (in 764).

While the frailty or accident of the human race frightens the last term of life by a sudden transposition, it is necessary that he does not find each one unprepared, but whoever wishes to receive the salvation of souls, it is necessary and fitting that he endeavors to redeem himself from his own things. Therefore, I, in the name of God, Egidius, considering the case of human frailty, determined that for eternal retribution or the remission of my sins I deserve to obtain forgiveness from the most merciful Lord in eternal bliss: I want to be a gift and a perpetual gift to the monastery of St. Salvator, which is built in the borders of Ardinna on the river Prumia, where the venerable man Asuerus the abbot and a large crowd of monks seem to have gathered, where I laid down the hair of my head for the name of the Lord: this is my villages called Caveniaco, Novavilla in the village of Celmanico with all the appendages, and whatever it seemed to me to serve there. In the same way, I give my villages called Nuilliac, Duciago, Flaviaco, Calviniaco, Juliaco, Caniaco, Cubicio, situated in the village of Rhodonicus, with all the appurtenances, or whatever looks to the towns themselves and it seemed to me to serve there, as a gift from the present day to the very house of St. Savior with all integrity. In the same way, and other things which I handed over to St. Salvator, I give to that very holy place, which my children, by these names, Aginaldus, and also Bertricus, or Botlenus, and Paulus, should cultivate through your presbytery, so that whatever sense [census] you see fit, you may attach to them, which they shall pay to you every year, and every one of them after his death, whatever he held in precariousness, with all things improved, shall return to the very house of God named above, with all integrity, into his dominion, without any confusion or contention: this is Comnis, Viva -water, Caihaco, Fol, Patriniaco, Altiaco situated in the village of Celmanico with all the appendages and all integrity. In the same way I give to Dono and the other towns named Calvono, Laviniaco, Averiaco, Aurudo, Serant, Colrido, Bron, a fourth part of Serant, Duniaco situated in the village of Andegavinse with its appendages and all its integrity. In the same way I give and other towns named Druvio, Palriciaco, Quevo, Bursinas, Piriallo, Dimisiniago, Cuptiago, Balatiago, situated in the village of Rodonicus with their appendages and all their integrity; and other things which we have not mentioned here above, or which I procured, or which my ancestors gave me, or which are to be sought for and found, I give to the very house of Saint Salvator, and they themselves from the present day, or whatever on the part of my parent Beririgi, and on the part It has come to me from my mother-in-law Viventiana, or from what has been acquired, or from what is known to have come to me, a gift with all its integrity, as well as lands, houses, buildings, farms, manors, vineyards, forests, fields, meadows, pastures, waters and watercourses, flour mills, with shepherds and herds of cattle of both sexes, mobile and immobile, whatever can be said or named, or whatever looks or seems to belong to the places named above from the present, with everything exquisite, I want to be given whole and intact to the very holy place from the present day and confirmed, so that from this day forth you may have free and firm power in all things to have, to hold, or to do whatever you may choose from thenceforth. However, I do not believe that will happen; if I myself, which is far from happening, or one of my heirs, or any opposite person, or anyone against this letter of my donation, which I decided to be done for the sake of the name of the Lord and the veneration of the holy place, should decide to come, or try to violate it, or a repeater of this has arisen, may he receive upon himself the wrath of God the Father, and the Son, and the Holy Spirit, and appear as a stranger from the thresholds of the churches, and from the association of the saints, and moreover bring to the parts of the monastery itself, forcing him to the treasury, 5 pounds of gold, 20 weights of silver. forced to pay, and what he repeats that no one should be able to claim, but that the present donation of my will at all times remain firm and inviolable, supported by a stipulation. Done at the public monastery of Prumia, under the 16th day of March, in the year 14th, in the reign of our lord Peppin, the most glorious king.

XXX. King Peppin's privilege for the monastery of St. Maximinus (in 765).

Having promised our Lord and Savior eternal life in the Gospel, we believe, with full and complete faith, without doubt, that we will be rewarded in the future age, if we strengthen the stability and tranquility of the monasteries, and increase the ecclesiastical affairs, giving to God, with protection. Accordingly, I, Peppin, king of the Franks, by the grace of God, declare in this testament to all future kings forever, that I have under the royal power a certain monastery, where the saint Maximinus, the proconsul of God, is buried in his body, built, that is, in the suburbs of Trier, and dedicated in honor of St. John the Apostle and evangelists, that the monastery with the treasury and the whole abbey should always be under the abbot of that place, because I hold that it has been found to have been established in this way by kings in former times. Wherefore I decree that this present abbot Utilradus, and all the abbots who shall come after him from the same place, together with the monks and abbeys, shall remain forever under the rule of the kings of the world, that they may be freed from all restlessness, and be able to serve God with spiritual joy. I also grant the election of the abbot to the aforesaid monks by royal authority, so that they may have the power to elect whomever or whomever they please, for the reason that he may keep the rule with his subjects. But if anyone, being absent, wills to break this charter, or cause any trouble to the family of the same place in any matter contrary to the will of the abbot, he shall incur the wrath of God, and shall be held guilty of the royal majesty at all times. And that this description may be firm, we ordered it to be sealed with a ring. Adolphe resigned. Given that he did the month of January. In the public palace (that is, of Ingelheim, not of Mainz) in the 14th century of our successful reign.

XXXI. Testament of Tellus, bishop of Curia (Anno 766.)

In the name of the Holy Trinity. When we wish to remember the mystery and the secrets of our hearts we must always remember the benefits of the Most High bestowed on the human race: when the Lord our God Jesus Christ deigned to come down from the bosom of the Father to redeem us, who even me, unworthy and least of all the servants of God, did not by my merits, but by his clemency he deigned to place me among the princes of his church; , which was given by our first parent, and the outcome of this uncertain life, and recovering hope, by the Lord himself graciously promising sinners that with alms, those who will can redeem their sins. I give his own, giving it to him, when he says through the prophet: The earth is the Lord's and the fullness of it. , or of St. Martin, or of St. Peter, whom we know were built in this place, or of other saints, whose names are built in this place: we know that a monastery of the regulars was built at the order of most of the servants of God in a place called Deserina, where I am unworthy, as if a sinner seems to possess Tello, a bishop, and I owe more than my expenses, I use it, or for washing my many sins or those of my parents, I donate and transfer to the very church of St. Mary, St. Martin, or St. Peter, that is, my grandfather To Jactati and my grandmother Salvia, and to my parent Victor, or to the illustrious governor and my mother-in-law Teusinda, or to my uncle the bishop of Vigilius, and to my brothers-in-law Zacconi, to Jactati and Vigilius, and to my nephew Victor and my sister-in-law Salvia, or to my nieces Teusinda and Odda. according to the scriptures, that he who possessed things of the church, or had something of his own property, the canons testify that he must associate with the things of the church: therefore I, a sinner ordained bishop, here confirmed by the above testimonies, give after my death or decease to the aforesaid sacrosanct church of St. Mary and St. Martin. or the census of St. Peter, which I establish and distinguish to be forever, and of my right to right, and to his dominion I deliver, and even transfer forever: this is the land or inheritance of my father Victor or the illustrious President, whatever he acquired by individual instruments of whatever acquired by my genius, and which the Lord has deigned to give me through his generosity: this is my court in Secania; in the first salam with the terrace under the fireplaces, above, other fireplaces under the cellar, the kitchen, the shelters, around the courtyard, the stables, the floors, the barns, or other hospitals, or cellars, and everything that pertains to the courtyard itself, all completely. Also, the curtain with its fruit trees. Likewise, the orchards and vineyards under the court in their entirety. Also in the castle, the walls of the hall under the cellars, the terracottas in the castle itself, as far as it legitimately belongs to me, everything in its entirety. Also, in the street, my court with the floors, with the barracks, with everything that belongs to the court itself, with his entrance from the whole. Also in the territories sixty-five modials of land to Buliu, bordering on the court itself, on one side to Saint Columbanus: ten modials of land across the Vic, bordering on Gallonicus, on the other side to Amanti: eighteen modials of land in Stava, bordering to Victoris, on one side of the road: land in Sarrs eighty modials, bordering on Sancti Columbani, on the other side of the road: land of Astireda fifty modials, bordering on Calausionis, on the other side to Vigili: land on the Rhine thirty modials, bordering on Lobeceni, on the other side to the Livings: forty modials of land in the Rhine, bordering on Jactati, on the other side to Urseceni: twelve modials of land in the same place, bordering on Pauli: two modials of land before the Sala: six modials of land below the Sala, bordering on the road: thirty Alevenoce modials, bordering on St. Columbani, with a cottage, with two floors, with its courtyard and entrance, and with its canine houses, bordering the field itself on the road: another field, ten modiales, bordering on Solemnis to St. Martin. At the top of Levenoce Roncale with its building from the whole: also, a meadow under the curtain under Secanius, and sixty burdens with its building, bordering on St. Columbani, on the other side of the road; Pradum in Heretis, sixty burdens, bordering on St. Mary's, on the other side on the road. Pradum in Levenoce, fifteen burdens, bordering on St. Columbani, on the other side in Vedalion, as much as I seem to have in Levenoce itself, in full. Also, in Alpe Agise burdens a hundred. Pradum in Castrices in Roncale, twenty loads, bordering on Agusti, on one side of the road. Pradum above the rocks of Roncale, thirty loads, bordering on Sancti Martini, on the other side in Vederanion. part to Lobonis. Also, in Flemme Roncale from the whole. Also, of the colonists of the very court of Secanius: Ariscio, Gaudentius, Exoberius, Calanho, Valerius, Anulfus, Crespius, Jactatus: all these with their wives and children, fields, meadows, and whatever it belongs to the colonies themselves, with all their whole stock. Also, of the Spehatici, Froncione Projectum, Evalus, Flechosvu, Lobecinus, Aurelius, Victor, Saturninus, Masson, Rusticus,

Desiderius, Lobucione. All these with their wives and children, fields, meadows, or all that pertains to the spikes themselves, together with all their bundles from the whole. Amantius in person except the land of Saint Mary alone, Auster with his brother, Aurelianus, Praestantius, Valerius, Viventius, Columba. All these with their wives and children and whatever they seem to worship, return as Priors. Likewise, my villa in Iliande, salam with the cellar, with everything that seems to be held in its entirety around the salam itself; torbaces, floors, bareca, courtyards, gardens, everything with its entrance; which seem to be held around the court itself, which legitimately belong to me in their entirety. The field under Lobene is sixty modiales, bordering on Sancti Martini: the field next to the court, fifteen modiales, bordering on Sancta Maria: the Aflupius field, six modiales, bordering on Quartini: the Roncale field six modiales: six modiales of land in front of Vicum, bordering on the road. Likewise, they will border the meadow in Campaniola, ten burdens. In Sanctae Mariae. in St. Mary's. Likewise, on the rocks, my farm with the cottage, with the floors, with the torbacs, with the garden, and all that pertains to the yard around it, in its entirety: a field, sixty modials: a meadow, a hundred burdens. another meadow to Naulo, forty burdens: let all these be given to the aforesaid church. Also, the colonists of the court itself Iliande, Sporcius, Vidalinus, these two with their wives and children, fields, meadows, and with all their land, and whole. Also, Despicus, Vidalianus. I add to the very monastery of St. Mary, or St. Martin, or St. Peter. Also, Muricia salam with the cellar, with the chimneys, with the terrace, with the barn, with the stable, with the barres, with the floors, the porch, the yard, and everything that belongs to the yard itself. with his entrance, all from the whole. Likewise, the land in Rouen, thirty-five modials, bordering on the river, on the other side in St. Mary's: the land in Rouen itself, four modials, and bordering on the Juliani, on the other side to Canis: the land across the river eleven modials , bordering on Projecti, on the other side on the river: land above Castellum, eight modiales, bordering on Silvioni, on the other side with Evalenti: land on the court itself, eight modiales, bordering on Juliani: land in Vorce, sixty modiales, bordering on Vicaoni, another part of the road with its building, with its yard and its entrance, everything completely.Also my yard in Selauno, with the floors, with the bareca, with the torbace, with all its appurtenances, and everything that pertains to the yard itself, completely.Also the field to Feniles, eighty modials, bordering on the court itself: the land of Arduna, sixteen modials, bordering on Evalenti, on the other side in Juventi: the land in Vicinave, seventeen modials, bordering on Lomeleng, on the other side in Sancti Martini: also the meadow at Sorella, eight onas, bordering on Lidori: meadow Anives in Curtino, twelve burdens, bordering on Abatissae: meadow in Esce, twenty burdens, bordering on Beravi: meadow in Colimne, five burdens: meadow on Rhine, twenty burdens, bordering on Victurucionis, on the other side to Juliani: meadow in Rouen, ten burdens, bordering on Saint Martin: four burdens of meadow in Vallecava, bordering on the road: twenty-five burdens of meadow on Macene, bordering on the road, on the other side of Crespion. Likewise, the colonists of the very court of Tauren: Laurentius and Lopus: these two with all their wealth, from the whole. De Selaune, Lidorius, Maurus, Befanius, Sicarius: all these with their wives and children, and with all their wealth, from the whole. All of these with their wives and children, with all their property from the whole. Also, from the court itself, Maurelius, Dominicus, Donadus: all these with their wives and children, the field, the meadow, or whatever belongs to the cottages themselves, all from the whole. Leo in person alone. Fescianus with his wife and children, lands, spoils, and with all his property, in their entirety: let all these return after our death to the very monastery of St. Mary, or St. Martin, or St. Peter. alone, standing with the apple-trees, as far as it legitimately belongs to me, except the land of the churches, my whole portion: and besides the colony which I granted to my junior Senator for his service in Maile itself. to his own, and whatever legitimately belongs to me, everything in its entirety. Likewise, the plain forest above Maile, as far as it legitimately belongs to me, be given and granted to the very monastery of Saint Mary, or Saint Martin, or Saint Peter. which we give to the monastery itself, which we have mentioned above, above Iliande, as far as it concerns me, in its entirety. with the rising, and whatever appertains to the court around it, with its entrance and exit, with the waters, with the pastures in the woods: also, Roboredum under the Rucene, from the whole. Also, the Alps, which we give to the monastery itself, which we mentioned above: with its successor, in full. In Fadohine, my portion in full. In Ceipene, my portion is full. Also, we determine about our faithful, to whom, as much as we have granted to us living, and after our death we give. he shall return after our death to the monastery itself with all its appurtenances: likewise, the land which Lidorius himself possesses. for everything that seems to have more than this number should return to the aforesaid monastery. Likewise, Alecus holds forty modials of land in Ilian himself, and he himself will return to the monastery itself after our death. Also, Gaudentius holds fifteen modials of land, and he himself will return after our death to the monastery itself. Also, Crescentianus holds a specie in Rucene, and four modials in the Rhine, and he himself returns, as above. Also, Leontius the chamberlain holds five modials from Helanengo: likewise, the presbyter Vigilius holds three modials from Helarinengo, and he himself returns to himself after our death monastery. Also, Goncio holds a field in Vorce, eighty modiales, and it shall return to the monastery itself after our death: also Vadardus holds a field of fifty modiales, he shall return after our death to the monastery itself: likewise Januarius holds two colonies in Tauronto besides men; and they shall return to the monastery itself after our death. Likewise, the colony held by the presbyter Silvanus, the fields, meadows, fields, gardens, buildings with all their appurtenances, and with our own servant, named Viventius, who lives in the very house: let all these things return after our death rum to the monastery itself. Also, the colonies which the priest Lopus holds in Falarie, one with a man, another without a man, fifteen meadows, a field in Roncalina, twenty modials: let all these return after our death, both slaves and land to the monastery itself. Also, a colony in The very Falarie, which Jactatus worships, we give to our junior senator both while we live and after our death to possess. Also, the colony which Amicho holds, she shall return to the church itself after our death. she shall return after our death to the monastery itself. Also, in Valendano Majorinus holds twenty-five modials of land, he shall return after our death to the monastery itself. food for his wife and children. That if he withdraws himself from that place, the possession itself shall remain stable in the monastery itself, and it shall not be permitted for anyone to withdraw it from it. Likewise, the land which Drucius holds in Castrice shall return after our death to the aforesaid monastery, and Drucius himself let us establish that it is a sacred place. in this world, let all things remain in my power, and after my death let this gift continue firmly, both in fields, meadows, sun, sunrises, buildings, mills, alps, forests, waters, pastures, accessions, vineyards, orchards, stocks, Major and minor, ironwork, ironwork, lacework, vessels, utensils, movable and immovable, all that pertains to the life of man, should be given and granted to the very monastery of St. Mary, or St. Martin, or St. Peter, which is called Desertina. (which we do not believe will be the case) that I (as far as it may be) or any of my heirs or pro-heirs, both male and female, or born of certain or uncertain, or pretended kinship, both relatives of my race and of my neighbor far away, or any foreign person, small or great, acting in judgment, care, or royal power, or someone who has been granted by royal power, or moved by the presence of dogeals, or by gifts of office, or by his own power, has believed himself foolishly proud, or has dared to withdraw from these churches, and contrary to this deed of ours, or of my parent, which he himself commanded to be done in this way, the commandment, that this registration of the property of our resources should be done, both of the compaction and of the property, of any kind of tract, or acquisition that has come to our knowledge We decided to have this establishment of the redemption of our sins, and the company of the saints to be sealed, because I unworthy, with a sound mind and a sober heart, while I was living, I took care to fulfill my father's precepts, my desires, so that for myself, and for all my parents who are written above, from the most high Judge we deserve to earn forgiveness for our sins. For this reason, I have appointed the Creator of the world to be judged intermediate, so that he may be aggressive against him who has dared to break in against this fact, or to try, or by any ingenuity presumes to generate slander against the churches themselves. In the first place he incurs the wrath of our Lord Jesus Christ, and is anathema by the holy Trinity, that is, the Father, and the Son, and the Holy Spirit, and in the same way on the day of judgment he descends to the left with the illustrious into the depths of hell, like Dathan and Abiron and Core , who had stood in rebellion against Moses, so he, like them, drowns himself in the abyss of the earth: and like Judas, the betrayer of the Lord, hangs himself in a snare, and obtains body and soul of the punishments of hell without end - and as much for our sins, and those of our parents, and the faithful Our divine mercy has graciously commanded him to forgive them, that the sins of all these may come upon him, and that he may receive condemnation with the devil and his ministers, and that he may appear as a stranger to the confederacy of the faithful Catholics. First, condemnation, separation from the saints. Second, rejection from the Lord's face. Third, immersion in hell. There they serve long and at night. And on top of all this, let him be guilty of twenty pounds of gold and forty pounds of silver, which he repeats, in any of his requests, but let him be, as befits, confused about everything. I, with a ready will and a devout mind, begged it to be done, unshaken at all times until forever, with the stipulation attached to it. many good witnesses.

+ *The sign of the hand of Lord Tellon, the generous bishop, who commanded these things to be done, and I confirmed them with my own hand.*
+ *The sign of the priest Silvanus the witness.*
+ *The sign of Justinian's hand as a witness to the judge.*

+ *Sign of the presence of a court witness.*
+ *The sign of Lobucion de Amede, a court witness.*
+ *The sign of Constantius de Senegaune, a court witness.*
+ *The sign of Lobucion de Maile, a soldier witness.*
+ *The sign of Paulus de Treminus, a soldier witness.*
+ *Signum Claudius de Curia curial witness.*
+ *Signum Urseceni de Scanavicus, a court witness.*
+ *The sign of Victor, the son of an eminent soldier, a witness.*
+ *Justinian's sign of Vico Meldon, a soldier witness.*

+ *The sign of Foscion of Pogius, a soldier witness. And I, priest Foscius, having been commanded by my lord the bishop of Tellon, wrote this donation, and signed it with my own hand.*

XXXII. The order of King Peppin, by which he restored the town of Exona to the monastery of St. Dionysius (in the year 766).

Peppin, king of the Franks, was an illustrious man. We believe that we associate with the eternal judge in reward, if we know this, that he was delegated to the places of the saints, and by the precept signed by the hand of the previous kings, we affirm there by confirmation through our oracles for the love of God, and the retribution of the saints. Therefore, the venerable man Folradus, the abbot of the special basilica of our patron Saint Dionysius, where the precious martyr himself and his companions seem to rest in the body, either the abbot himself seems to be living together with a large company of monks, or they are known to the military Lord, suggested to us in a sent petition that Clotharius, king of the Franks by his precept he had delegated to the very house of Lord Dionysius a town called Exona, situated on the river Exone in the Parisian town: and afterwards Chlodius, king of the Franks, had reconfirmed it again to the basilica itself by his precept: whence he shows us the precepts themselves to be relegated, where we find that through unjust greed afterwards the village of Exona itself was taken from the house of St. Dionysius, or diminished, by malicious men. The abbot himself, or the congregation itself, has pleased the majesty of our kingdom, that by our confirmation or our deliberation we should emanate such a precept, that just as it was possessed by Count Remehon through our benefice, with all its boundaries or appendages, so with all integrity to the monastery itself or the monks serving there, or the lighting of the church itself, or the wages of the poor, the aforesaid town should make progress there in increase, and that he may better choose the monks themselves for us, either to our brother Kallomagno of good memory once, or to our subsequent descendants, day and night more attentive to the Lord's mercy to apologize Therefore, the aforesaid town with all the public taxes, and with the lands, houses, buildings, accolades, mancipi, vineyards, woods, fields, meadows, waters or streams, movable and immovable, flour mills, as we have said above, with all integrity a part of the aforesaid monastery and its governors let them have, hold, and possess, and to the very house of God in our alms or in our kinsman it should be confirmed in full right for ever without any repetition. And in order that this cession may be more firmly established, we have under-confirmed it, or endeavored to seal it with our ring.

The sign of the most glorious king Peppin.

He recognized Baddilo in the name of God.

Given publicly in the month of July, in the fifteenth year of our reign, the city of Aurelian. Itherius wrote happily. Amen.

XXXIII. Donation of Peppin to the monastery of Saint Antoninus (in 767).

The treasonous and forbidding notices carried out by Sir Peppin, the Most Serene King of the Franks and Aquitaine, in the presence and hand of Fedancius, abbot of the church of Saint Anthony the Martyr, which is situated in a valley called the Noble, where the border is known to be in the village of Ruthin.

To this tradition, religious men were witnesses [...] of the abbot of Fedanci, namely Hildebald, the archbishop of the see of Rem, and also Aimarus, the archbishop of the see of Bituric, together with a group of other bishops numbering twelve, among whom was Justinus, the bishop stricken with a royal disease, who prostrated himself before the altar where his head he was guarded by the most glorious martyr of St. Antoninus, he was suddenly protected by divine protection and by his intervention he was freed. At the same time there was a company of soldiers and counts, among whom was Count Bertalargus, Wulfrandus, Botelinus, Counts Paletinus, and others in number of sixteen. They all agreed with one voice and did not applaud with the greatest crowd of people who were there, that the house of God was worthy to be enlarged for the love and reverence of the blessed Antoninus the martyr, who always stood as the defender and protector of the king and all his army. To their acclamation, Peppinus, the most serene king, obtained to enlarge the house of God by royal gifts. And so, with his advisers, the magnates, the monastery of St. Peter the Apostle, which is called Mormacus, which is situated in the village of Catucirno above the river Avarion, he gave into his own possession the head of the blessed Antoninus the martyr, and the altar, in which he rests with the honor and blessing of God, and to the abbot Fedancio, a venerable man and monks. and to the present and future clergymen living there. The entire aforesaid monastery and its adjacencies, that is to say, together with the other two churches, one of which is Mornagallus and the other the chapel of the holy martyr Felix, as well as the monks and servants and all the possessions that belonged to it, and in the future, the Lord nodding, will be given away ; with vineyards, orchards, cultivated and uncultivated lands, watercourses and watercourses, vats, and mills, which gave all beyond the river 81 cubits from the border of Mount Cusson to the middle of the ear and to the mouth of the ancient vessel. As much as is enclosed within those boundaries, whole and from the whole, he gave to the proper adobe of the aforesaid house of God. As for the repetition, if any emperor or king or leader, count or vice-count or abbot, or any person great or small, wishes to withdraw the aforesaid from the house of God; let him be smitten with the sword of the aforesaid bishops, and be buried with Dathan and Abiron in hell.

Dated the 2nd of the month of April in the 16th year of the reign of Peppin the Most Serene Emperor.

Sigiltredus wrote.

XXXIV. King Peppin's decree by which the town of Autmundistat is given to the Fulden church (in the year 768).

Peppin, king of the Franks, was a illustrious man, and because, as the Scriptures admonish, it is necessary to constantly prepare each one so that when he comes before the heavenly Judge he deserves to hear that pious voice of the Lord, with which all the righteous will be happy from good deeds, therefore we are healthy, as we believe, considering how from earthly things we God's mercy has been deigned to bestow upon us abundantly in this world, at least we should give it to the poor from this, so that we may be able to receive his mercy. some non-concerning Autmundistast, which is placed in the village of Moinigangio on the river Riechina with all its boundaries or appendages, so that with all integrity the monastery itself or the monks serving there or the luminaries of the church itself or the wages of the poor should be procured there, the aforesaid town should advance in growth and that it may be better loved the monk himself, for us, or our brother-in-law, or the next of our descendants, to pray more attentively day and night for the Lord's mercy; Therefore, the aforesaid town together with the lands, houses, buildings, acolytes, servants, hedges, fields, meadows, pastures, waters, and watercourses, movable and immovable, as we have said above, with all the integrity whatever at the present time seems to be our possession there, is part of the aforesaid monastery, and the abbots of this monastery have . and in order that this cession may be more firmly established, we have secured it below, or endeavored to seal it from our ring.

The sign + of the most glorious king Peppin.

In the name of God Baddilo recognized and signed.

Given in the month of July in the fifteenth year of our reign, the act of the city of Aurilion was officially written in the name of God by Hitherius.

XXXV. A letter from the house of Siegfried in Alsace to his son Altmann, in which he assigns most of his goods to the Gregorian monastery (in the year 768).

To my dearest and most loving son Altmann.

I, Sigifrid, in the name of God, thinking for the love of God, that I had given you my things in the village of Alsace; at the end of the Heiderheim mark, and in the village or at the end of the Tessinheim mark, and in the town of Tuginisheim, which is in the Heruncheim mark, and at the very end of the Heruncheim mark, from the forest, from which he can fatten fifty pigs, and in the very Heruncheim mark from the meadows, from which he can cut one hundred and thirty cartloads of hay, excluding those particles which we have donated through God's huts. Again, I give the things named above, both cottages and curtilages, buildings, manors, vineyards, lands, fields, meadows, woods, waters, and watercourses, by gift and transfer. If I myself, or on behalf of my heirs and heirs, or any contrary person, who tries to come against this tradition, or wants to break it, shall be the first to incur the wrath of God.

Acted officially in the town of Heruncheim. The sign of Sigifrid who asked for this tradition to be made + the sign of Luitghero + the sign of Sighimund + the sign of Marcold + the sign of Siwalfu + the sign of Horseninus + the sign of Eborninus + the sign of Raffal + the sign of Bero. Given what he did to God on Sunday on the 8th of the month. In the 18th year of August, in the reign of Sir Peppin, the most glorious king.

I, Hurulfus, an unworthy sinful priest, have written and subscribed to this tradition.

XXXVI. The decree of King Peppin, by which the Aequal forest is granted to the monastery of San Dionysian (in 768).

Peppin, by the grace of God, king of the Franks, is an inglorious man, to all agents, both present and future. It must be desirable to earn eternal from transitory things, or to spend from perishable substance in order to gain eternal joys. Therefore, considering the same matter, we donate to the basilica of St. Dionysius, where his precious body rests with his holy companions, and Fulradus the abbot seems to be presiding, and donated forever for the remedy of our souls, or also for the burial place of my body, to be in the same holy place we want, this is our forest known as Aqualina, with all its merit and solidity, whatever looks or seems to belong to the forest itself, as it has been possessed by us until now. Therefore, by this precept we command more particularly; and we want it to be perpetually established, as the already-said forest of Aqualina, with all its integrity, whatever inwardly or outwardly looks there: that is to say, both the manors, the lands, the houses, the buildings, the accolades, the estates, the woods, the vineyards, the fields, the meadows, the pastures, the waters, or the streams, movable and immovable, money, savings of both sexes, flocks with herdsmen, as well as different kinds of beasts, or also foresters with their own dwellings in the forest itself in different places: that is, the Cotonarias (Couvières) with all integrity, and those dwelling in Ulfrasiagas two, and Humlonarias with integrity; Likewise for Visiniolo, likewise for Ursionevillare; in Putiolis (Puisieux) two manors, and Adsumumbragium with all its integrity, except half a manor; and one manso in Villarcellus (Villarceau); in Brogarias one remained, and in Actricomonte with integrity, and likewise in Asbertovicinium, two remained in Villare (Villiers); in the Popiniagas I stayed one, and in the same way in the Valley: everything and from everything, as we have said, completely and completely except so much as it is known to have been previously granted to the places of the saints by means of charters; that is to say, to Saint Germanus of Paris, and to the cell called Fossatis, which is situated in Parisiacus itself, and to Saint Benedict of the monastery of Floriac, and to the Church of Saint Mary in the city of Carnot, and to Saint Mary of the Argentogel monastery, and to Saint Peter of the Church of Pectavens; part of the aforesaid monastery from the present day to receive perpetual possession. But the boundaries of the forest itself are as follows: on one side the above-mentioned Cottoniaria, and Watreias, and Sarnetum (Sernay), and the old monastery; on the other side Epaneville, and above the writing of Putiolis and Rumbelitto (Rambouillet); on the third part Hermolitus (Hermeray); therefore from the fourth part Adtaneville (Attainville) and Burdoniaco (Bourdonné) and Condato (Condé) and Vitriaco; then on the fifth part Pincionemonte (Montfort) and Villare. All these above included, from this day the governors of the holy place shall have, hold, and enjoy the aforesaid wood of Aequalina under the name of amenity, and in the use of the monastery itself. Nevertheless, we wish and command that no presumption of judicial power for certain occasions, or to exercise any hunting, without the permission of the rector of the monastery itself, should at any time presume that a penitent should not enter there under the same boundaries, but as we have granted in our alms, so it should be preserved forever in every way. But which precept, in order that it may be more firmly established, we have decided to confirm it below.

The sign of the glorious king Peppin.

Hitherto I reviewed and signed.

Given in the month of September, in the seventeenth year of our reign. Acted successfully in the monastery of St. Dionysius.

XXXVII. The decree of King Peppin concerning the immunity of the monastery of St. Dionysius (in 768).

Peppin, king of the Franks, was an illustrious man. At the beginning of our kingdom, I watched with affection for our erection, fully assisting the Lord, and for the very good works we should have increased with the counsel of the Pontiff, or with the immunity of our senior nobles, for our strengthening the kingdom and the mercide, or the fishing of the adine, we should renew our eternal life: which we did so. Therefore it is necessary for Clement, the chief among other requests, that which is ascribed to salvation, and is demanded for the divine name, to receive a placating hearing, and to bring it to fruition beyond doubt, inasmuch as the eternal is sought from the transitory things of the present age, according to the commandment of the Lord who says: Make friends of the mammon of iniquity. (Luke 16:9). Therefore, according to what he said about the mammon of iniquity, we must purchase eternal heavenly things. and while we are imparted to the proper benefits of the priests, from this we deserve to have the retributors to the Lord in eternal tabernacles. Therefore, the venerable man Fulradus, the abbot, from the basilica of the special patron of our lord Dionysius the Martyr, where the precious lord himself rests in body, begged the Clement of our kingdom that for a long time all immunity from the towns of the aforesaid Saint Basil had been granted by the predecessors of the kings. he asserts that he has in his hands, and this he asserts that it has been inviolably preserved until now: wherefore he asked that this be done again on our authority for the firmness of the matter, concerning the very holy place, or of the man who, if their substance should deliver him to the basilica itself, or pardon him, according to the fact that the previous kings by their authorities they performed and confirmed this at the basilica itself, we should grant and confirm this by repeating it about the abbot himself. Therefore, let your greatness or usefulness know that, out of reverence for the holy place itself, or for the sake of rest, the promptest will of those worshiping God there once more granted, and confirmed in all things, let your skill know. Wherefore, by this precept, which we decree more particularly, and wish to remain in perpetuity, we order that neither you, nor your juniors, nor your successors, nor any one girded with judicial power, enter the courts of the aforesaid holy basilica of Lord Dionysius, wherever and wherever, into any villages in to the kingdom of God, by our propitiation, that at the present time a part of the monastery seems to possess or rule, or that it was granted there by God-fearing men by lawful means, or that it was previously added to, and destroyed, neither to hear cases, nor to remove the sureties, nor to demand peace , neither to make lodgings, nor to be ready, nor to require any recompense, to enter, nor to demand at any time at all, shall he be completely presumptuous, unless whatever our treasury could expect from thence, everything and from all, as a summary of our wages, with all colds granted in full, so that it has been said, if we look at the very precepts of the former kings, or according to what our present authority seems to contain, whatever the holy place itself seems to have at the present day, as we have said, than what has been added or contributed to it there by God-fearing men, or by us, or to whomsoever justly and reasonably, when he has surrendered all his possessions to the monastery itself, and has delegated or secured his affairs there by legitimate instruments, may he be able to reside in complete immunity for the present day, quiet and secure; . to implore the mercy of our Lord more attentively. And in order that this authority may remain firm and inviolable throughout the ages, and may be better believed by all judges, we have endeavored to outline it with our own handwriting.

The sign of the most glorious king Peppin.

Hitherto I reviewed and subscribed.

Dated on the ninth of the month of October in the 17th year of our reign. Acted in the very monastery of St. Dionysius.

XXXVIII. Peppin's order confirming the privileges of the monastery of St. Dionysius (in 768).

Peppin, king of the Franks, was an illustrious man. At the beginning of our kingdom I watched with affection for our establishment, the Lord helping us completely, and for his good work, I acted with the advice of the priests, or of our senior nobles, for the strengthening of our kingdom, and for a reward, or to obtain eternal life, and for the reverence of Saint Dionysius, the martyr, Rusticus, and Eleutherius. , who by a glorious and triumphant vow for the love of Christ obtained the crown of martyrdom, to their basilica, where they seem to rest and shine in miracles, to the monks themselves, who seem to serve there, living regularly under evangelical freedom, as the ancient fathers or previous kings confirmed, we should once more renew the privilege of our office in the very holy place: which we did. Therefore, the main clemency among the rest of the petitions, that which is ascribed for salvation, or is requested for the divine name, must be accepted by a placating hearing and brought to effect, so that there may be a conjunction in the reward, while the petition is imparted for the peace of God's servants or the congruity of venerable places. Therefore, while the almighty Father, who said that light should shine out of darkness, through the mystery of the Incarnation of his only-begotten Son, our Lord Jesus Christ, or the illumination of the Holy Spirit, shone into the hearts of the Christian saints, for whose love and longing among the other glorious triumphs of the martyrs, blessed Dionysius, and often The already mentioned Rusticus and Eleutherius, who were the first after the apostles, under the ordination of blessed Clement, the successor of Peter the apostle, arrived in this province of Gaul, and there preaching the baptism of repentance for the remission of sins, while they were contending in this manner, there they earned the palm of martyrdom and received glorious crowns: where by many times and even now in their basilica, in which their bodies seem to rest, Christ deigns to work not the least miracles of virtue for them: in which also lord Dagobert, once king, seems to rest, may we also, through the intercession of their saints, merit in the heavenly kingdom with all the saints to participate, and to perceive eternal life. Therefore, the venerable man Folradus, the abbot, believed it to be suggested concerning the very basilica of the particular patron of our lord Dionysius of the clemency of our kingdom, that a long time ago an entire privilege had been granted by the priests of the city of Paris to the very basilica of lord Dionysius, and confirmed by our inner kings from that time until now: who affirms that he has the privilege itself, or the precepts or confirmations themselves, before his hands; but for complete firmness the man Folradus, the abbot himself, requested from our highness that we should affirm this repeatedly by our precept. Let your greatness discover that he most willingly accepted such a religious request and confirmed it in everything. But since the temple itself, or the holy place itself, seems to have been enriched with things by the above-mentioned princes, or by other ancient kings, and by God-fearing Christians, because of the love of God and eternal life, our complete devotion is, as we intimated above, a privilege to the holy place itself. we ought to make or confirm to the abbot or brethren consistent there for future quiet, that it may be more easily permitted to the congregation itself to pray regularly at the thresholds or at the tombs of their own martyrs for the stability of our kingdom. We, therefore, by this series of our authority, according to what was done by the aforesaid privilege by the priests, or confirmed by previous kings, for the reverence of the martyrs themselves, confirm, as it were, to the very holy place both in towns, manors, or in whatever things and bodies from the ancients by princes, or by God-fearing men, because of the love of God, it was delegated there, or it was afterwards added, while also from the munificence of kings, as we have said, the holy place itself seems to have been enriched or founded, so that none of the bishops, neither present nor those who were to come, were their successors ordinators, or any person, may not by any order take away anything from the place itself, or usurp any power for himself in the monastery itself, or anything like the title of exchange without the will of the abbot himself, or the congregation himself, or our permission, and neither chalices, nor crosses, or It shall not be permitted for them to take away the vestments of the altar, or the sacred books, or the gold, or the silver, or any kind of specie, of which it has been brought there, or to be given, taken away, or diminished, nor to carry them to the city at all, nor presume to do so: but it is permitted to the holy congregation themselves, or themselves to possess forever the holy place which was conferred upon them by right delegation. In this privilege of our serenity it was decided to insert that, when the abbot was summoned from the very house of God from this world by the divine nod, the holy congregation from the monastery itself should be allowed to choose from among themselves, and whom they found good and worthy, who would bear the very burden of the abbey according to the holy order may rule or govern, and if they unanimously agree, given authority by us or by our successors, an abbot should be installed there in the very house of God, and for the stability of our kingdom, or for all our laws, or for the safety of the country, may they constantly be able to implore the Lord's mercy. Because we, for the love of God, or for the reverence of the holy martyrs themselves, and to obtain eternal life, we were seen to have performed this beneficence to the holy place itself, or to the monastery itself, by the consent of the priest, aristocrats, illustrious men, our ancestors, with the most gracious spirit and complete devotion. or that he had granted, that is to say, in order that, as in the time of the former kings, the psalmist was set up there in the holy basilica itself by troupes, as the holy order teaches, it should be celebrated day and night perpetually in the holy place itself. Which authority, supporting Christ in all of us, we trust because he helps those who consent to him, and despises those who wish to destroy him. And that it may obtain firmer vigor, and that it may be kept unharmed by the help of God in our times and in future times, and that it may be preserved through the ages, we have endeavored to outline it with our own hand.

The sign of the most glorious king Peppin.

Dated on the ninth of the month of October in the 17th year of our reign. Acted in the very monastery of St. Dionysius.

XXXIX. Diploma of Peppin, king of the Franks, in which Fulrado, abbot of St. Dionysius and his chaplain, confirms the tradition made to him by Widon, dynast of Alsace, in Gemar, St. Hippolytus, Ensheim, Schaeffersheim, Grusenheim, and Rappolsweiler. Dated September 23, 768.

Peppin, king of the Franks, an illustrious man. To all our bishops, abbots, or counts, or nobles, and messengers running everywhere from our palace. And since we are seen to govern the kingdoms of the earth by the mercy of God, we must constantly weigh them in the name of God, in so far as our propitiation protects those whose concern seems to have been entrusted to us, how we also protect those who need protection, and support them in the right path. For especially in these our honor must shine unceasingly, who not only seem to keep the faith they have received towards us in everything, but also do not cease to devote themselves to the service with all their united strength. And therefore, we think it right, that those who are known to exercise such things, and in our times should make their lives lead peaceful, and in the future, by the firmest right, those which have been granted by us, without restlessness, with free powers, Christ the Archangel, should be able to rule in all things. Therefore, while it is known to many that he has been discovered, it is evident that he was connected to the faithful God's propitiation and to the venerable man Fulrado, our chaplain or archpresbyter, who arrived before these days for the cause of labor and was close to death. And therefore, handing over to us the things of his property, which a certain man named Wido had delegated to him, that for his soul we should confirm the very things to the holy places. But since, by the help of divine mercy, he was again restored to his former health, we were again seen to have delivered the aforesaid things to Fulrado himself. But he himself believed, as if through a certain space of time, for the love of lust, some men should demand the things just aforesaid, or for that very reason should generate slander against him; therefore he asked our highness that, instead of the tradition itself, we should generally confirm our precept on the same; know that he also provided for us with a grateful heart, or strengthened us in all things. For as the aforesaid venerable man Fulrado, our chaplain, is commanding the very things which the said Wido delivered to him, that is to say, Ghosmari, Audaldovilare, Ansulfishaim, Suntor, Grucinhaim, Ratberto Villare, or whatever the aforesaid Wido appears to possess through Fulrado himself, which the aforesaid Wido has delivered to us, with all integrity, both lands, houses, buildings, farms, manors, vineyards, forests, fields, meadows, pastures, waters, water courses, movable and immovable, money, savings of both sexes, flocks with shepherds, or all goods, regardless of the amount of the paternal, or from his mother's side, or from wherever it is known to have descended from Widon himself in legitimate order, whatever he appeared to have in Alsace and Mordenaugia; all and to the whole, which was his possession in the very villages, and he delivered them to Fulrado, and he, as we have said above, delivered them to us in his weakness, and we again delivered them to Fulrado himself; from this day onward, out of our generosity, he should have the license to have, to hold, to give, to sell, to exchange the things themselves; even if, for the love of Christ and for the remedy of his soul, he wishes to delegate the very things to the places of the Saints, wherever it pleases him, by our permission, without any disturbance of the judgments or the treasury, or by the refusal of the heirs of Widon himself, he may have a free and firm control in all matters concerning them. the power to do whatever he wants. But what authority, that it might be more firmly held, or better preserved through the ages, we fixed under it, or sealed it with our ring.

A sign to Peppin the most glorious king. He quickly recognized and signed.

Given on the ninth day of October in the year 17 of our reign. Acted in the very monastery of St. Dionysius.

XL. The decree of King Caroloman, the brother of Charlemagne, by which he confirms the immunities of the Dionysian monastery and the exemption from taxes for all those attending the festival or the market of St. Dionysius (year 769).

Carloman, king of the Franks, was a illustrious man. To all the bishops, abbots, dukes, counts, domestics, vicars, centurions, or all agents, both present and future, or all our messengers running everywhere. Therefore, let your usefulness or greatness know, because the venerable man Fulradus, abbot of the particular basilica of our patron Saint Dionysius, where the precious lord himself seems to rest in his body, or the abbot himself seems to dwell together with a large company of monks in the same convent, or they are known as a military lord; they suggested to us in a mass petition, because the lord and father of good memory, Peppin, once king, or other predecessors who before him or us held the governorship of the kingdom of the Franks, through their oracles and their strengthened hands, granted such a boon to the house of St. Dionysius, below the village of Paris, on that festival Saint Dionysius, our patron, in the same, or through the towns, or through the fields, both there and elsewhere to negotiate or carry out many negotiations, or to procure wines in the ports and by different rivers, who have arrived for the festival itself: that he himself they would have granted or confirmed in full from the very turn to the house of St. Dionysius below the village of Paris. Wherefore the precepts themselves of the aforesaid, and the judicatures or confirmations of the former kings (as has been inserted above) have now been offered to us for reading: the very precepts or and confirmations read and perused, either by that judgment vindicated by the lord and father of good memory Peppin once king, or Childebert, as well as Grimoald of the elder house, whom the agents of St. Dionysius claimed over the agents of the previous judges, offered themselves to us for relegation. And afterwards Fulradus himself, or the monks of St. Dionysius, suggested, and this they said, that the tax-collector of him in their towns or fields should be present without judges at the entrance to the house of Lord Dionysius; He declares that he reported through his hands to our father Peppin, the most glorious king, either how it had been the custom of kings there for a long time, or whether he himself was granted or preserved tolls at the very house of God. And while they had found acts or perpetrated in this way by previous kings, they presented us with such precepts or confirmations to be read. And once again we granted, that from this day no one by judicial power, neither in the marque itself, nor through their lands, nor their ports, nor of their people, nor of their traders, nor of all the nations whatsoever, who come to the aforesaid marque, nor through their villages, neither of the boats, nor of the ports, nor of the carts, nor of the sails, with any toll, nor foratic, nor rotary, nor bridge, nor portatic, nor salutatic, nor cispitatic, nor mutatic, nor any exact custom, nor any four dinars from all the nations that come there to the very marque, which the Counts of Sonachildis and Guaireridus (as we have mentioned above) used to send, to kill them, not below the very village of Paris, nor the city itself from the same turn, nor anywhere else who come to the festival itself. Neither you, nor your juniors, or your successors, shall demand any exact, or contrary, nor presuming to exact, unless (as we have said) whatever our treasury may have hoped for from our side, or even from all our agents, everything and from all himself let the tolls to the very house of God be granted in full and pardoned or vindicated: so that in future times they may have it confirmed or vindicated by our authority either of previous kings, because we for God's sake and reverence for the aforesaid saint Dionysius the martyr, or for our souls the remedy or stability of the kingdom of the Franks. or to our ancestors and to their posterity this in lights to the very house of St. Dionysius, or to the monk himself, or to the poor and the stranger, in our alms we have granted or confirmed this in all: that it may please them better for the stability of our kingdom, or for all our joys, keeping in mind the mercy of the Lord to plead, and that he may progress to the very house of God in ever and ever-lasting times in increase. And that this confirmation of ours may be held more firmly in view of the precept itself, or more judiciously vindicated to the lord Peppin, the king, or to other kings, and to be preserved perpetually around the very house of God; We decided to sign it under our hand, and to seal it under our ring.

A sign to Charles the most glorious king.

I recognized Maginarius and signed.

Given in the month of January, in the first year of our reign. Act of Salmunciago in the public palace in the name of God successfully.

XLI. King Charles's charter for the monastery of St. Gregory (year 769).

Carloman, by the grace of God, king of the Franks, a man of insolent count Garinus, we believe that it belongs to us beyond doubt in the name of God to the stability of our kingdom, that we bring to fruition the petitions of priests or churches, in which they have been brought to our ears, and therefore he knows greatness or usefulness, because a venerable man Restoino, the abbot of the monastery between the two Pachinas, for our fee from our treasury near Aufold, out of our full and complete grace, we granted such a benefit and guaranteed such a benefice, that no matter how much the men of our fiscals could procure, or by any contract they could add or attract, this is our serenity about the monastery itself We ought to confirm the vile abbot of Restoin himself and his successors in general, for they command that neither you nor your juniors or successors should exist completely contrary to the same, except what we have said, no matter how much [,,,] written by the abbot of Restuin out of our munificence than from what was procured, or from any kind of attraction to add to or attract to the monastery itself [...] there would be no fiscal on our part required of him from this, unless it is permitted to him for part of the monastery itself under the immunity title of both the abbot [...] for their successors to live and dwell in peace, that they may choose better for the stability of our kingdom. . . and to exhort ours, and in order that this precept may obtain fuller force, we have resolved to strengthen it by placing our hands and seals upon it.

I recognized Maginarius and signed.

A sign + given to Carloman the most glorious king under the 11ᵗʰ of the month of April, in the first year of the reign of our lord Charles, the most glorious king. Attiniago's palace in the name of God was successful.

XLII. The decree of King Carloman concerning the immunity of the church of Argentoil (in the year 769).

Charles, by the grace of God, king of the Franks, a illustrious man. For it behooves a king of clemency to bestow convenient benefits upon his faithful, and to secure the effect and faith of what he has demanded of the righteous. Having desired the favors which our predecessors are known to have been cancelled, we wish to confirm for our oracles in the same, that they may the better choose to serve faithfully towards our government. Therefore, in Christ the Lord, Sagrat Ailina, abbess of the monastery of Argentolaius, addressed the Clements of our kingdom, suggesting that our predecessor, the former king, having strengthened their hands through their authority, had granted or established a judge in the whole of the towns of his church without entering, so that neither the public judge nor to act, nor to demand fridas, nor to build mansions, nor to demand any recompense from the villages of the aforesaid monastery, whatever our treasury could receive therefrom, should not enter. Wherefore she affirms that she has the precept of our forefathers in her hands, while she herself in the present offered to be banished, and it was a boon granted to her by the kings themselves, to be asserted or preserved by them at the present time. But for complete firmness he asked our highness that our authority should be more fully established around this. But let us know the usefulness of your greatness, that for the love of God you have confirmed or granted us this favor once more with the fullest will. Accordingly, therefore, we order that, while the aforesaid monastery had its hands strengthened by the king's own predecessors by their precepts, or the abbess of Ailian, who has already been mentioned, was completely protected from all her towns without the entrance of the judges, that they seem to preserve this benefit from the same at this present time and in the future, neither you, nor your younger successors, nor any judicial power in the courts of the monastery itself, or of the abbot of Ailina, which has already been mentioned, nor to act, nor to demand fridas, nor to make mansions, nor to require any recompense, whatever our treasury could hope for, ingest, or demand it is not to be presumed, unless by our indulgence it remains perpetually unmoved. And so that this authority may continue to be firm, we have decided to strengthen the seal below with our hand.

A sign + to the most glorious king, Lord Carloman.

Given in the month of November, in the second year of our reign. Acted at the public palace of Pontion, in the name of God, successfully.

LXIII. Carloman renders justice to the monastery of Prumien from the place of Benutfeld (Anno 770.)

Charles, by the grace of God, king of the Franks, a illustrious man. Indeed, let us implore the royal clemency and pray for the hearts of our faithful, if, concerning those who have exercised unfaltering faith and true fidelity both to our father and to us until now, their petition in which they have revealed to our ears, and the hearts of those whom we now have in our possession delightful and lovable, we know that every day we are more cheerful and prompt about our service. And therefore, faithful, by God's propitiation, our illustrious man Dirodoinus, count of our palace, made known the clemency of the kingdom to God as our adjutant, saying that our ancestors once, kings appointed by God, through the instrument of a series of charters, to his genealogy or his subsequent descendants, through their authorities, and their hands they had indulged in the reinforcements or confirmations of the kings, and had confirmed in their right power a certain forest in a place called Benutfelt, below the hundreds of Belslang, below the vast Ardennes, and of the surrender of the kings in our presence he brought back the very forest to be sacked, and informed us that the executioners were unjust the forest itself had been partly invaded, and my father Peppinus, the most glorious king, had made the aforesaid Dirodoinus or his followers of Gamaladion clothed with their own hands from the forest itself, while the account of this cause was thus brought before us, and his own or that of Gamaladion's both by untruthful men, and by confirmation [confirmations] we knew of the kings, we render justice to him about the place called Benezvelt, about that fountain which is in the town itself, below each of them should have a part as far as it pertains to us; a vein from the fountain itself in the circuit through different places, which on our part our judges unjustly contradicted themselves. We order that from this day the forest itself is part of our parts already mentioned, as well as in future times, so that no public judge should at any time take away from our parts, nor diminish, nor contradict the same forest below, the same vein on each side, as well in the forests and in the lands, fields, permits, plains, meadows, pastures, waters and watercourses, adjoined, adjacent, all and from all under integrity, as we have already said, should be owned by Dirodoinus himself or his Gamaladion, as well as their posterity, and cleared, and whatever they wish to do with the forest itself, they shall have, hold, and possess by our authority, and leave it to their posterity to possess, as we have said, and from then on they shall have the free and most firm power to do whatever they wish by our authority. And in order that this authority may be more firmly established, or better preserved through the ages, we decided to strengthen it under our own hand, and to seal it with our own ring.

The sign of the glorious king Carloman. I recognized Mainarius.

Given in the month of May in the second year of our reign.

The act of the Brocmagad palace was successful in the name of God. Amen.

XLIV. The charter of Charles of Austrasia, king of Austrasia, by which he confirms the goods of the monastery of Honaugi, dated in March 770.

Charles, by the grace of God, king of the Franks, a illustrious man. To all the bishops, abbots, dukes, counts, domestics, vicars, centenarians, or all our missionaries, both present and future. Knowing that we believe that the most important fortification of our kingdom will increase, if we grant appropriate benefits through the benevolent deliberation of the local churches, we trust that the Lord will continue stably under his protection. Therefore, let your wisdom know that we have been seen to have indulged ourselves at the request of the venerable man Stephen the abbot for eternal retribution, so that, etc.

The sign + of the most glorious king Carloman. I recognized Maginarius and signed.

Given in the month of March, in the second year of our reign.

Deed of Theudoneville in the public palace, in the name of God successfully.

XLV. A charter of Charles of Austrasia, king of Austrasia, which confirms to the monastery of Noviente, or Ebersheim, the goods which Adalric, duke of Alsace, had granted to the same monastery. Dated May 6, 770.

Therefore, by the grace of God, king of the Franks, an illustrious man; and because we have learned from the testimony of Scripture that the king who sits on the throne of judgment destroys all evil with his glance, therefore we believe that it will be fulfilled by us, who manage the care of such a great name, if we endeavor to enrich and sublimate the venerable places of the churches of God with the advantage of any gift, and that to ourselves We have no doubt that it will benefit our state and kingdom. Therefore he knew the sagacity of all the faithful of God and of us, both present and future, such as Isenhardus, abbot of the monastery, whose name is Noviento, situated in a village in Alsace above the river Illa, whose husband was the illustrious leader Adalricus or Atticus, and his wife Bersvinda in the name of Christ and in in honor of the holy apostles Peter and Paul, and of Saint Maurice the Martyr and his Companions, who had built anew in their own land, he appealed for the clemency of our kingdom, begging for the privileges which, in pious memory, our father Peppin and his predecessors, that is to say, kings of the Franks, in the same monastery and places that They contributed to the support of the brothers who serve God there, we will renew. We therefore proceed by the authority of his royal majesty, confirming the constitutions of our predecessors, as to the villages which the aforesaid leader gave as a dowry to the church of the aforesaid monastery with all their appurtenances, that is to say, the churches, the fields, the fields, the buildings, the cultivated and uncultivated lands, the acrolas, the mancipias, the meadows, pastures, forests, hunting, watercourses, fishing, mills, roads and entrances, exits and returns, quests and inquiries, or in any way named interests pertaining to the property itself he delegated, that is, in Wishuvilare, which is situated in the village of Brisigaugensi above the bank The river Rhine with all its appendages. In Sulza with all belonging to him; in Burchheim, in Lagelenheim, in Gruzenheim, in Sigoltesheim, in Racenhusen, in Oleswilern, in Scerenwilere, in Sarmeresheim, in Hudenheim, in Northus, with every tenth of their estates. No public judge, no judicial power, presumes to enter, neither to bind any of the people there, nor to hear cases, nor to remove the cold, nor to make lodgings or preparations there, nor to demand anything from our treasury. But the aforesaid abbot Isenhard, and his successors, may possess the same property by increasing and improving it. And in order that this our authority may remain firm and inviolable, we have set our hands under our signatures, and have sealed our ring under it.

The sign of Lord Carloman, the most glorious king, in the name of Christ. I recognized Maginarius and signed.

Given on the ninth day of May, in the second year of our reign.

The act of Bruocmagad was successful in the name of God. Amen.

XLVII. Charlemagne's privilege for the monastery of Grandisvallen (in 770).

Charles, by the grace of God, king of the Franks and Lombards. Let it be known to all the bishops, dukes, abbots, counts, domestics, vicars, centurions, or all those running about our missions. Whenever the right request of the priests, which will be beneficial for the opportunities and the holy places, has come to the ears of our clemency, such must also be heard or actually commanded in the name of the Lord, from which we deserve the forgiveness of the eternal retributor, and he will choose them to continually plead for the stability of our kingdom, or in to assist our kingdom faithfully in every part. Therefore let your greatness or usefulness know that the monastery of Grandevalle, built in honor of St. Mary the virgin, and the Cella Verteme in honor of St. Paul, and the Cella of St. Ursicinus the confessor, under his subjects, where the venerable man Gundoaldus seems to preside, he made known by mass petition, by the fact that our father of good memory, King Pepin, or the other kings of our ancestors, who before him or us held the helms of the kingdom of the Franks [...] and their hands being strengthened, yielded such a boon to the said house itself, that their towns were completely exempted from its merits, according to their perceptions , which our predecessors conceded from the power to the house itself, they perceived full and complete [...] or rather we were seen to have conceded it to their said successors.

Wherefore by this our special precept we have decreed, we order, that it shall be perpetual [...] granted, that neither you [...] nor yours, nor any one girded with judicial power, in the courtyards or villages of the monastery itself or in their buildings looking thereto by any villages and territories, as much as he seems to possess or dominate at the present time, and that he may still increase, improve, or attract from the office of kings or queens, or from the contributions of the people, or from those obtained, or from any kind of things, to hear cases, and not to exact , nor to remove the officers of the faith, nor to make men or women ready, nor to distrain men, nor to distrain their ministerial servants or servants, or the acolytes of the monastery itself, nor to require any public repayments, nor to exact them. As to whether it will be returned to our treasury or to the counts from thence, let the judicial power, nor our envoys, presume to run away, unless all their towns are under the name of immunity; when all the concessions were granted, or the public refunds were granted, everything was comprehended as above. Both Abbot Gondald himself and his successors may at all times be able to possess and rule this in the name of the Lord. As for the monasteries or monks themselves; those who are there or presided, we have granted such an increase of our remuneration, that no rebuttal of what is contained above, which was granted to them by our clemency, neither in ours nor in future times, or at any time at all, so that this should not be done except that for this it was granted by our command, that it should remain perpetually unsullied and unmoved. And in order that this our authority may be more firmly established, and better preserved in all things through time, we have signed our signatures below and sealed it with our ring below.

XLVII. The charter of King Carloman, in which he grants the towns of Faberola and Noronto to the Dionysian monastery (in the year 771).

Charles, by the grace of God, king of the Franks, a illustrious man. And because the Scripture admonishes that it is necessary for each one to be constantly prepared, to the extent that when he comes before the heavenly Judge he deserves to hear that pious voice of the Lord, whence all the righteous will be glad of good deeds; therefore, as we believe, considering how well we are able to give from earthly things, which the heavenly grace has deigned to bestow upon us abundantly in this world, we should at least give from this to the poor, so that we may be able to obtain the mercy of the Most High. For this reason, we surrender and donate for the remedy of our souls, or for our father Peppin the late, to the monastery of St. The very house of God had long ago delegated, called Faberolas, which is situated in the village of Madriacense, and Noronte in the village of Carnot, with all their integrity, or their appendages, to the monastery itself, or to the monks living there, or to procure the lights of the church itself, or the stipends of the poor, as aforesaid that the villages should advance in increase, as they were possessed by our vassal Audegarius, and that the monks themselves should be better chosen to implore the Lord's mercy day and night for us and for our father. Therefore we give up and donate the aforesaid towns of Faberola and Noronte to the holy place, together with the lands, houses, buildings, farms, farms, vineyards, woods, fields, meadows, pastures, watercourses and streams, movable and immovable, flour mills, flocks with shepherds, all and from all, as we have said, with all integrity, whatever appears to be our possession there at the present time, shall be a part of the aforesaid monastery and its governors to have, hold and possess perpetually in our and future times, and to the very house of God in our alms forever without any the repetition must be fully confirmed by law. And that this authority may remain firm and unshaken, we have confirmed it under our own hand, and have commanded it to be sealed with our ring.

A sign to Charlemagne, the most glorious king.

I recognized Maginarius and signed.

Given in the month of December, in the fourth year of our reign.

Act of Salmunciago in the public palace, in the name of God successfully.

XLVIII. The Testament of Remigius, Bishop of Argentina, or the Charter of the Donation of the Monasteries of Aschovia and Wertha to the Church of Argentina. March 15, 778.

In the name of the Father, and of the Son, and of the Holy Spirit, under the day of March, in the tenth year of the reign of our most glorious lord King Charles. Therefore I, Remigius, though a vilest sinner, a servant of God's servants, by the grace of God bishop of the city of Argentina, with a sound mind and a sound plan, made this testament which I composed with full devotion and single will, which I myself dictated and wrote and signed with my own hands, using a legitimate number of witnesses. who, at our request, have signed below, or strengthened the seals with their own hands, that I want the testament to obtain the most complete firmness for the turn of all the codices; and if, on account of the civil law of the praetorium, someone wishes to invalidate the intestacy, and so that it is not valid, witnesses shall be given to this heir of my sacrosanct church, and to my lady Mary, the mother of God our Lord Jesus Christ of Argentina, where the mercy of God or the mercy of the holy Mary will have the honor of pontificating me he ordered Therefore, my sweetest lady, holy Mary, I appoint you to be my heir, and I choose and decide in everything, and I commend to your protection everything that has been decreed by me, and which are contained below written in this testament, you most pious and sweetest lady before the God of heaven and You have the supreme power to fulfill and complete the will of my land in all things. Therefore you, my sweetest lady, Saint Mary, since God has commanded me to leave this light and fragile body with his vocation, you, lady, assist me as an heir. Therefore, to you, my sweetest lady, my heir, Saint Mary, I wish to be a gift and gift to you forever, on the basis that, as long as God gives me space to live, and Scholastically to my niece, or Rederam to my great-nephew, whatever I was seen to have in the village of Alsace, on the island called Hascgaugia, on the river Ila, and the island itself is in the march of Blabodsaim, and in the march of Quibilisheim, with the basilica above it, which I built anew and consecrated, where I buried my lady Saint Sophia, and gave her most precious body a place of burial, which Lord Adrianus, the supreme pontiff, gave me to serve, and I myself carried it from the city of Rome to this region on my shoulders with my ministers with great decorum. Therefore, my sweetest lady and heir, Saint Mary, I give you the body of Saint Sophia; I also commend the very church which we have dedicated in honor of St. Trophimus, where St. Sophia herself rests in body, together with the island of Ascgaugia itself, which Roduna, the religious of God, and Adala, the abbess, have handed over and pardoned portions of the island itself to us and to St. Sophia, or letters before They confirmed the witnesses. Therefore, sweetest, I give to you, and my heir, Saint Mary, I hand over to you the very island for the remedy of my soul, or for eternal retribution, so that I may earn eternal forgiveness from the pious Lord. And you, my most pious lady, deign to entreat for me the Lord Jesus Christ, whom you deserved to bear in your womb, that he may grant me eternal forgiveness as a sinner. Therefore, my sweetest lady and heirs, I give you the island of Aschaugia above mentioned with all integrity and solidity, with basilicas, with houses, buildings, courtyards, orchards, manors, vineyards, woods, meadows, fields, lands, fields, farms, pastures, and savings of both of the greater and of the lesser sex, and of servants, and of savings, with waters and streams of water, or whatever may be said or named, and there seems to be my legitimate possession there today, and whatever seems to look towards the holy place itself, and condoned there by good men through a series of writings it was, and whatever I acquired there, was either handed down to me, or I acquired it through the title of comparison. And I have again delegated to you, my sweetest lady, Saint Mary, by the title of donation, to the very holy place, in that manner, as we wrote above, we hand over and pour out, so that you yourself may be worthy to intercede for my sins, so that I may receive forgiveness, and reduce the amount of my sins; In the same way I give to you, my sweetest lady and heir, in another parcel of the monastery of Aragougen, which is called Werith on the river Araris, and it is the very island of Grechchinbach, which bishop Rapertus built from a new work, and he himself handed it over to me with his knife in the presence of witnesses, and again to the Germans. He was captured by these names. Ertulphus and Cundbertus requisitioned the monastery itself, and I then redressed them. But afterwards, thanks to God and to the interceding good men, and to my Xenius that I gave, or my favor that I bestowed on them by way of precarity, while they themselves lived, and from then on they paid us the rent, and after their death we would restore our dominion and the favor itself, this is , which was the property of Raperti from the alode, and by this the Germans of Raperti handed over the monastery itself to us again in the presence of witnesses, or they also made a charter of the surrender to us, and they covered the monastery itself with us, and by means of a feast they made their exit from the monastery itself in the presence of witnesses, as It was the law of the Alamanni. Therefore, to you, my most sweet lady and heir, Saint Mary, I give you the very monastery called Werith, and it is in honor of Saint Leodegarius the martyr, at the end of Grechchinbaccen, on an island above the river Ararim, both for the salvation of my soul and for the remedy of the soul of the raptured bishop. that you yourself may intercede for us, that we may deserve to be helped by God, that our offenses may be blotted out, and that we may deserve to receive everlasting forgiveness from the pious Lord. Therefore, to you, my sweetest lady and heir, my holy Mary, I give the monastery named above with all integrity and solidity, with basilicas, with houses, buildings, with all the adjacent and appendages, with villages, courts, curtifers, mansions, lands, territories, mancipi. It was delegated by good men to Leodegarius, the holy place of God, by charters of tradition and grant and sale. To you, my sweetest and heir, Saint Mary, I hand over to you all these things named above, and pour them out, in that manner as we have said above. That I myself, and my niece Scholastica, and my great-nephew Raderamnus, while we lived, by your favor, my lady, and my successors, who seem to be at that time, should have under usufructuary, and a tax every year at the festival of Saint Mary at the dedication of the altar itself. which we have just dedicated, we must give 20 solids in silver, and we want this, that our canonical clerics may receive the same solids there in our alms, so that they may choose better to serve God and Saint Mary day and night, and to pray to God for us, and that our names be written may they be in the book of life, and that my little body may rest in that crypt, which I have made with a new work. I will, and I pray, and I beseech, and I charge my successors, that you may by no means have permission to cast out my niece Scholasticus, nor my abducted nephew Raderamnus, from the very benefit which I have given, that is, that cell of Saint Sophie on the island of Aschaugia and in that monastery in Aragaugia, which is called Werida. And if you contemn these things, or wish to do anything else, except what I have written above, you will then bring an account before the judgment seat of Christ, and you will not be able to do this. And when, indeed, when I, Remigius, and Scholastica, and Raderamnus, have already fulfilled the office of fate, you, the most holy Church, holy Mary, and your agents, whole and entire, as it was possessed by us, shall recall to your power and dominion, and to you perpetually, holy Mary, our heir. may he prosper in growth. And this we wish and beseech, that after the departure of ours, no man may at any time have in favor those cells of Ascgaugia and Werida, which I have given to Saint Mary. If anyone and any person, at any time, by any means whatsoever, contrary to this testament, which I made of my own free will, inspired by the divine mastery, and which I myself wrote, should attempt to come or act, or will to be contrary, or to diminish, or to break through, the wrath of God will come first. he incurs, and from the forefather, who is at that time, he exists excommunicated before God and holy Mary, and on that terrible day when the district examiner arrives, the guilty and judged depart, and moreover he brings to the holy administrators in the sacrosanct church of Saint Mary my heir, together with the most sacred treasure, pounds of gold five, the weight of silver is forced to pay twenty-five, and what he repeats is not worth claiming, and nevertheless the present page of the will must continue with firm stability, supported by a stipulation. Act of Argentine citizenship. I have noted the day and year above.

I, in the name of God, Remigius, a sinner, and by the grace of God, bishop, have read this testament made by me in love of holy Mary, which I myself wrote with my own hands, and which I asked to be written above.

The Scriptorium Project is the work of a small group of lay people of various apostolic churches who are interested in the preservation, transmission, and translation of the works of the early and medieval church. Our efforts are to make the works of the church fathers accessible to anyone who might have an interest in Christian antiquities and the theological, philosophical, and moral writings that have become the bedrock of Western Civilization.

To-date, our releases have pulled from the Greek, Syriac, Georgian, Latin, Armenian, Indo-Persian, Germanic, Nordic, Slavic, Celtic, Ethiopian, and Coptic traditions of Christianity, and have been pulled from sundry local traditions and languages.

www.ingramcontent.com/pod-product-compliance
Lightning Source LLC
LaVergne TN
LVHW061040070526
838201LV00073B/5116